# THE ALCHEMY OF STARS

# THE ALCHEMY OF STARS

## *Rhysling Award Winners Showcase*

edited by Roger Dutcher
and Mike Allen

Science Fiction Poetry Association

Published by the Science Fiction Poetry Association
in cooperation with Prime Books.

For more information on the SFPA:
www.sfpoetry.com

For more information on Prime Books:
www.prime-books.com

"A Dream of Heredity" by John Calvin Rezmerski. Copyright © 1986 by John Calvin Rezmerski. Originally appeared in *Tales of the Unanticipated* #1, 1986.

"egg horror poem" by Laurel Winter. Copyright © 1998 by Laurel Winter. Originally appeared in *Asimov's Science Fiction*, July 1998.

"Eighteen Years Old, October Eleventh" by Joe Haldeman. Copyright © 1990 by Joe Haldeman. Originally appeared in *Asimov's Science Fiction*, Aug. 1990.

"Encased in the Amber of Eternity" by Robert Frazier. Copyright © 1979 by Robert Frazier. Originally appeared in *Future at War Vol. 1: Thor's Hammer*, Ace Books, Reginald Bretnor, ed. 1978.

"Epitaph for Dreams" by G. Sutton Breiding. Copyright © 1989 by G. Sutton Breiding. Originally appeared in *Narcopolis & Other Poems*, Hell's Kitchen Productions, Peggy Nadramia, ed., 1989.

"Epochs in Exile: A Fantasy Trilogy" by Charles Saplak and Mike Allen. Copyright © 2002 by Charles Saplak and Mike Allen. Originally appeared in *EOTU Ezine*, Feb. 2002.

"Explaining Frankenstein to His Mother" by John Grey. Copyright © 1997 by John Grey. Originally appeared in *Star*Line*, Vol. 20 #3, 1997.

"Fatalities" by Duane Ackerson. Copyright © 1978 Duane Ackerson. Originally appeared in *The Eggplant & Other Absurditites*, by Duane Ackerson, Confluence Press, 1978.

"Flight is for Those Who Have Not Yet Crossed Over" by Jeff VanderMeer. Copyright © 1993 by Jeff VanderMeer. Originally appeared in *The Silver Web* Winter/Spring 1993.

"For Spacers Snarled in the Hair of Comets" by Bruce Boston. Copyright © 1984 by Bruce Boston. Originally appeared in *Asimov's Science Fiction*, April 1984.

"For the Lady of A Physicist" by Michael Bishop. Copyright © 1978 by Michael Bishop. Originally appeared in *Black Holes & Other Marvels*, Fawcett Books, Jerry Pournelle, ed., 1978.

"Future Present: A Lesson in Expectation" by Bruce Boston. Copyright © by 1995 Bruce Boston. Originally appeared in *Asimov's Science Fiction*, March 1995.

"Grimoire" by Rebecca Marjesdatter. Copyright © 1999 Rebecca Marjesdatter. Originally appeared in *Tales of the Unanticipated* #20, 1999.

"How to Make a Human" by Lawrence Schimel. Copyright © 2001 by Lawrence Schimel. Originally appeared in *Half Human*, Scholastic Press, Bruce Coville, ed., 2001.

"In Computers" by Alan P. Lightman. Copyright © 1982 by Alan P. Lightman. Originally appeared in *Science 82*, June 1982.

"In the Darkened Hours" by Bruce Boston. Copyright © 1988 by Bruce Boston. Originally appeared in *The Nightmare Collector* by Bruce Boston, 2 A.M., 1988.

"January Fires" by Joe Haldeman. Copyright © 2001 by Joe Haldeman. Originally appeared in *Asimov's Science Fiction*, Jan 2001.

"Just Distance" by Roger Dutcher. Copyright © 2003 by Roger Dutcher. Originally appeared in *Tales of the Unanticipated* # 24, July 2003.

"Letter from Caroline Herschel (1750-1848)" by Siv Cedering. Copyright © 1984 by Siv Cedering. Originally appeared in *Science 84*, June 1984.

"Matlacihuatl's Gift" by Sonya Taaffe. Copyright © 2002 by Sonya Taaffe. Originally appeared in *Dreams & Nightmares* 63, 2002.

"Meeting Place" by Ken Duffin. Copyright © 1980 by Ken Duffin. Originally appeared in *Asimov's Science Fiction* November 1980.

"The Migration of Darkness" by Peter Payack. Copyright © 1979 by Peter Payack. Originally appeared in *Asimov's Science Fiction*, Aug. 1979.

"My Wife Returns as She Would Have It" by Bruce Boston. Copyright © 2000 by Bruce Boston. Originally appeared in *Asimov's Science Fiction*, March 2000.

"The Neighbor's Wife" by Susan Palwick. Copyright © 1985by Susan Palwick. Originally appeared in *Amazing*, July 1985.

"The Nightmare Collector" by Bruce Boston. Copyright © 1987 by Bruce Boston. Originally appeared in *Night Cry*, Spring 1987.

"Octavia is Lost in the Hall of Masks" by Theodora Goss. Copyright © 2003 by Theodora Goss. Originally appeared in *Mythic Delirium*, Winter/Spring 2003.

"On the Speed of Sight" by Ray DiZazzo. Copyright © 1981 by Ray DiZazzo. Originally appeared in *Uranus* #3, 1981.

"Pilot, Pilot" by David Lunde. Copyright © 1994 by David Lunde. Originally appeared in *Star*Line*, Vol. 17, #6 1994.

"Potherb Gardening" by Ruth Berman. Copyright © 2002 by Ruth Berman. Originally appeared in *Asimov's Science Fiction*, Dec. 2002.

"Rocky Road to Hoe" by Suzette Haden Elgin. Copyright © 1987 by Suzette Haden Elgin. Originally appeared in *Star*Line*, Sept. 1987.

"Salinity" by Robert Frazier. Copyright © 1988 by Robert Frazier. Originally appeared in

*The Magazine of Fantasy & Science Fiction*, Feb. 1988.

"Saul's Death: Two Sestinas" by Joe Haldeman. Copyright © 1983 by Joe Haldeman. Originally appeared in *Omni*, Feb. 1983.

"Shipwrecked on Destiny Five" by Andrew Joron. Copyright © 1985 by Andrew Joron. Originally appeared in *Asimov's Science Fiction*, May 1985.

"Skin of Glass" by Dan Raphael. Copyright © 1994 by Dan Raphael. Originally appeared in *The Kore* #2, 1994.

"The Sonic Flowerfall of Primes" by Andrew Joron. Copyright © 1979 by Andrew Joron. Originally appeared in *New Worlds* #216, 1979.

"Song of the Martian Cricket" by David Lunde. Copyright © by 1991 David Lunde. Originally appeared in *Asimov's Science Fiction* Dec. 1991.

"Spacer's Compass" by Bruce Boston. Copyright © by 1993 Bruce Boston. Originally appeared in *Specula* by Bruce Boston, Talisman, 1993.

"Spotting UFOs While Canning Tomatoes" by Terry A. Garey. Copyright © 1996 by Terry A. Garey. Originally appeared in *Serve It Forth: Cooking With Anne McCaffrey*, Warner Aspect, Anne McCaffrrey & John Betancourt, eds., 1996.

"The Starman" by Duane Ackerson. Copyright © by 1977 Duane Ackerson. Originally appeared in *Cthulhu Calls*, Vol. 4 #2 Oct.1976.

"Storybooks and Treasure Maps" by Steve Eng (writing as John Bredon). Copyright © 1978 by Steve Eng.

"To Be From Earth" by William J. Daciuk. Copyright © 1992 by William J. Daciuk. Originally appeared in *Xizquil* #7, 1992.

"Two Sonnets" by Helen Ehrlich. Copyright © 1983 by Helen Ehrlich. Originally appeared in *Science 83*, May 1983.

"Variants of the Obsolete" by Margaret B. Simon. Copyright © 1994 by Margaret B. Simon. Originally appeared in *Xenophilia* #9, Feb. 1994.

"We Die As Angels" by William John Watkins. Copyright © 2001 by William John Watkins. Originally appeared in *Asimov's Science Fiction*, May 2001.

"The Well of Baln" by Ursula K. Le Guin. Copyright © 1981 by Ursula K. Le Guin. Originally appeared in *Hard Words & Other Poems*, by Ursula K. Le Guin, Harper & Row, 1981.

"White Trains" by Lucius Shepard. Copyright © 1987 by Lucius Shepard. Originally appeared in *Night Cry*, Spring 1987.

"why goldfish shouldn't use power tools" by Laurel Winter. Copyright © 1997 by Laurel Winter. Originally appeared in *Asimov's Science Fiction*, Dec. 1997.

"Will" by Jane Yolen. Copyright © 1992 by Jane Yolen. Originally appeared simultaneously in *The Magazine of Speculative Poetry*, Spring 1992/Midsummer's Night Press Broadside, 1992.

"Winter Solstice, Camelot Station" by John M. Ford. Copyright © 1988 by John M. Ford. Originally appeared in *Invitation to Camelot*, Ace Books, Parke Godwin, ed., 1988.

"Your Time and You: A Neoprole's Dating Guide" by Adam Cornford. Copyright © 1982 by Adam Cornford. Originally appeared in *Velocities* #1, 1982.

# *Contents*



## The Rhysling Winners

# Foreword

## *Roger Dutcher*

Over twenty-five years ago I saw the ad in *Locus* for the formation of the Science Fiction Poetry Association (SFPA). At the time I had only just started combining the poetry I wrote with the SF concepts I loved. I had become a SF fan early in my reading life, and came to poetry only later. I found in poetry the same sense of wonder I found when I first read Ray Bradbury, Arthur C. Clarke and J.R.R. Tolkien.

Now, it is hard to believe I have been involved with SF poetry for over twenty-five years. Not because I don't have faith in science fiction poetry, or I don't believe that organizations can survive, but just because it is surprising that it has the staying power it has had. And how quickly the time has gone by.

Our small field is an intersection of two groups, poetry and science fiction, both large and well established. We have not been adopted by either of those two groups. Our members appear to come from the SF side of things, for the most part, which makes the "mainstream" poets wary. And SF has never really had any affinity for poetry although some of the genre's biggest names (Wolfe, Zelazny, Haldeman, Le Guin, Blish, Yolen, and many others) have written poetry and its major magazines (*Asimov's*, *Amazing*, *Omni* and even *Analog*) published SF poetry. It has been the poets of SF (and its relatives, fantasy and horror) that have made it a lasting genre.

Whether you trace the history of SF poetry to *Gilgamesh*, the ancient Greek poets and their world of gods who affect the lives of humans, the tale of *Beowulf*, or the archetype of Arthur, there are touchstones for SF poetry throughout the history of poetry. If we are to say Shelley's *Frankenstein* is the first SF novel then perhaps Byron and his "Darkness", with its apocalyptic theme, from the start of the industrial age, is the precursor of today's SF poetry. There is also Poe, whom critic Mark Rich points to as the father of speculative poetry for his ability to " . . . divorce . . . poetic reality from our consensus reality-making." However you chart the lineage, there was certainly SF poetry before the Science Fiction Poetry Association. Still, the formation of the SFPA was a key step in helping genre poets to communicate, to develop their own language, and to uncover their history. This anthology, though small, stands as an important representation of the growing body of literature that is science fiction poetry.

In addition to the winning poems in this anthology, we also encourage you to seek other science fiction poetry to read. The SFPA website at www.sfpoetry.com lists not just the winners of the Rhysling but the other nominees and where they appeared. We hope you will find these poets and read their work, and discover the books and magazines that publish SF poetry, all of which hold more poets to discover. These books, and the others mentioned in this volume, can be borrowed from your local public library, most likely via Inter-Library Loan (ILL.) We hope you will consider joining SFPA as well (see website listed above for details.)

An anthology is not produced by any one person. I am indebted to the many people who made this collection possible. Special thanks is due to co-editor Mike Allen, who made the publishing contacts and set the pace with his enthusiasm during the final stages of the anthology production. Thanks to Jane Yolen and SFPA founder Suzette Haden Elgin who provided our Introduction and Afterword, respectively; they also provided advice and guidance. Thanks also go to David C. Kopaska-Merkel, who was there from the beginning to the end with counsel and advice. Bruce Boston for his unstinting support and assistance. Robert Frazier for his Primer, his historical data and his support. Drew Morse, Deborah Kolodji, and Scott Green (who as then-President of the SFPA approved this project) have made valuable contributions. Ursula K. Le Guin, Joe Haldeman, Bud Webster, Sandra Kasturi, Karen Romanko, Lawrence Schimel and Davey Snyder also lent support and advice. The entire membership of the association has supported the project. I, of course, wish to thank all the poets who allowed their poetry to appear here, and the editors and publishers who have supported these poets, and all the other poets, by publishing our poems over the last twenty-seven years. I am glad to count so many of the people I have met in the SFPA as friends. Thank you all.

A special note: We were unable to obtain permission to reprint Thomas M. Disch's poem "On Science Fiction", which won for Long Poem in 1981. The poem appears in *Nebula Awards Stories 17*, edited by Joe Haldeman, and in the seminal speculative poetry anthology *Burning With a Vision*, edited by Robert Frazier. We recommend you seek it out.

— Roger Dutcher, Beloit WI, April 2004

# Introduction

## *Jane Yolen*

When in January 1978 Suzette Haden Elgin founded the Science Fiction Poetry Association, an award for the best speculative poetry was established at the same time.

The award was appropriately called the "Rhysling" after the famed bard from Robert A. Heinlein's short story "The Green Hills of Earth." Rhysling, known as the Blind Bard of the Spaceways, is clearly a man in a science fiction story, but his poetry—songs, really—harken back to a rhymed and metrical bardic tradition, which makes the name perfect for an award that honors both science fictional and fantasy poetry.

As Rhysling sings: *We pray for one last landing,*
*On the globe that gave us birth;*
*Let us rest our eyes on fleecy skies*
*And the cool, green hills of Earth.*

Though rhyme and metrics abound in much speculative poetry, many of the Rhysling winners are less obvious and less consciously archaic in their poems. The subject matter of the winning poems has ranged over the years, from computers, starships, and the speed of light, to Daedelus, Camelot, and a horror poem about a carton of eggs waiting to be eaten. Speculation, and fine writing, are the key to the prizes. The poets are not Kipling wannabes, but range in taste and artistic heritage, and in the winners one can find perfect sonnets as well as blank verse, and everything in between.

Why, one might ask, give an award specific to speculative poetry? Surely most poetry could fall under that rubric, being full of metaphoric language. And aren't we in danger of further ghettoizing speculative fiction by giving it an award all to itself? Two important questions, neither with an easy answer.

First, though a great deal of poetry may have a touch of the speculative—think of Donne's "Goe and catch a falling star..." or Yeats' "What rough beast...slouching towards Bethlehem to be born"—such metaphors do not necessarily make the poem part of our genre. Intent to deal with the sfnal or fantastical or horrific is certainly an important starting place. And while several of Yeats' poems, like "Wandering Angus," could be counted towards a Rhysling were they just being published today, mythical and mystical poetry was once more acceptable by the mainstream than it is today. But there is also an interesting shorthand in modern speculative poetry, a particular acceptance of a quirky set of rules and assumptions, like FTL flight or the co-dependence of virgins and unicorns.

Second, the ghettoization has already occurred. Poems in genre magazines are rarely seen outside the readership. Small chapbooks of horror poems or sf poems may sell at cons, but will never make mainstream readings. And in a world where there are cowboy poetry associations, haiku associations, awards for children's poetry and romance poetry and African-American poetry and a three day conference at Duke University Medical Center on "Poetry and Healing," an award for speculative poetry is a step forward, not a step back.

Members of SFPA can each nominate two poems from the previous year for the two awards—a long poem of fifty lines or more, and a short poem of up to 49 lines. Winners have included such recognizable names as Gene Wolfe, Ursula K. Le Guin, Joe Haldeman, Lucius Shepard, and John M. Ford. But the majority of winners are for poems by folk whose major contribution to the field has been in poetry.

And what poetry it is! Poems that are stirring, or puzzling, or challenging, or horrifying; poems that make the reader laugh or gasp or smile in satisfaction.

Oh yes, I won one, too. For a poem about my father cast as the wolf in Red Ridinghood. I hope it makes you shiver—and think. I hope it lasts in your memory.

—Jane Yolen, written on my 65th birthday

# Alchemical Post-Its
## A Rhysling Primer

### *Robert Frazier*

Science fiction poetry suffers from an identity crisis. It will suffer through eternity.

As a three-word label for a small sub-set of two great and distinct literary forms, "science fiction poetry" offers a firm grip on what you are reading in *The Alchemy of Stars*. The label is handy, yes, but clunky as all hell. How do you reconcile using the words fiction and poetry in such proximity? Which form does it adhere to the most? The problem is insignificant, but it generates debate among poets.

Let's clarify one thing. Foremost, a science fiction poem is a poem. It looks like one. It feels like one. When you turn the handle on an SF poem, it goes ping, not rattlety-trap rattlety-trap bidda bang bong. Unfortunately, a genre category for fiction writing has been cobbled on, yet we also employ less-than-ideal terminology when we invoke concrete poetry or cowboy poetry as a label.

Okay, I can live with a smidgen of split personality, but further inquiry seems prudent. Does the term signify some deeper schism? Does the field of science fiction poetry face re-evaluation? In my opinion, yes to both.

Before I offer some vague conclusions, let's take a look at the history of SF poetry, the tradition of the Rhysling Awards, and the poetics involved.

You can point toward the *Odyssey* and Tennyson and Blake and Poe and any number of precedents, but for all intents and purposes, science fiction poetry existed in a dormant state until the latter Sixties, when poetry began regular appearances in science fiction publications on both sides of the Atlantic. To cite two of several high profile examples, poems were consistently collected in the *Best of Fantasy and Science Fiction* anthologies, and England's *New Worlds* devoted space to serious works.

In 1969 a small poetry magazine entitled *Kinesis* emerged from the SF workshops held at Milford, PA, and included work by many of the participants in a brief three-issue run: Thomas M. Disch, Sonya Dorman, Ursula K. Le Guin, Marilyn Hacker, Gene Wolfe, and editor Virginia Kidd to name a few.

Also at that time, contemporary poets from the United Kingdom, raised on science fiction and the promises of technology, began to explore both inner and outer space using science as a metaphor. All three poets in *Penguin Modern Poets* #11—D.M. Black, Peter Redgrove, and D. M. Thomas—offered such speculations in 1968, as did Edwin Morgan in 1969 in *Penguin Modern Poets* #15, but the works of Thomas most explicitly referenced SF themes like androids, lifeforms on distant planets, etc. His personal collection from 1968, *Two Voices*, seemed to break hard ground...partly because it gathered several of the *PMP* science fiction poems with other major non-SF works (thus the "two voices" of the title poem accrued another level of meaning), and partly because it contained what many consider to be *the* landmark SF poem, "The Head-Rape," set in a future when telepathic humanity has created devices and taboos insuring mental privacy.

> and she could not help but see, he re-
> re-felt his lust, being carboned in her brain,
> she re-re-felt the hysteria
> that he re-felt, so he re-re-re-felt—
> Their bedroom infinite: two facing mirrors.

This poem was reprinted in 1969 by editor Edward Lucie-Smith in the anthology *Holding Your Eight Hands, An Anthology of Science Fiction Verse*, and, along with the inclusion of pieces like "In Sobieski's Shiel" by Morgan and "A Vacation on Earth" by Disch, it solidified *HYEH*'s position as a holy text for the next crop of science fiction poets that emerged on the landscape. With the support of John Fairfax's *Frontier of Going* (Panther, 1969) and Robert Vas Dias's *Inside Outer Space* (Doubleday, 1970), enough modern SF poetry was available to readers to set the stage for the Seventies.

## Ah, the Seventies

It was a time when poets explored science and science fictional themes with fresh zeal.

Edwin Morgan collected *From Glasgow to Saturn* in 1973 and *Star Gate: Science Fiction Poems* in 1978, and he wrote about the former volume in the *Poetry Book Society Bulletin* (#77). "Another group of poems is perhaps best described as science-fiction, though I would regard these as natural extensions of the imagination in an age of science. The poet, I think, is entitled to set up his camp on other worlds than this, and to bring back what he can in the way of human relevance."

With professional SF magazines and original book anthologies offering, on occasion, equal billing to poetic works, and, too, an expanding number of small press SF publications shifting focus toward poetic content, it can be said that science fiction poetry truly emerged from the shadows in this decade, emerged from its previous role as page filler or comic relief in the field. Even mainstream literary magazines like *Pacific Quarterly* and *Edge* featured special issues with SF poetry. The interchangeable term speculative poetry also emerged as a trimmer, more inclusive umbrella for other fantastical poems that stood beside SF works in many publications, including surreal, experimental, dark horror, and pure science poems.

"In the time since this material was first gathered," wrote Duane Ackerson about his SF poetry anthology *Rocket Candy: Speculative Poetry* (Dragonfly Press, 1977), "several magazines devoted to speculative poetry have appeared. I had not seen the term "speculative poetry" used in print, though it stuck me as a much apter and less awkward phrase than "science fiction poetry." The appearance of a magazine called *Speculative Poetry Review* has confirmed my suspicion I was on the right track."

The watershed years are easily pinpointed: 1977 and 1978. A small sample from this 24-month span contains single-author collections like *Windows & Mirrors*, Michael Bishop (Moravian Press); *Tomorrow May Be Even Worse*, John Brunner (NESFA Press); *Shooting Scripts*, Adam Cornford (Black Stone Press), *Spaced*, David Calder (Toulouse Press); as well as pure science poets Diane Ackerman with *Wife of Light* (William Morrow) and Loren Eiseley with the delayed and posthumous *All the Night Wings* (Times Books). Bellevue Press, who later published collections by Disch and Jack Dann, issued an SF poetry postcard series with short works by Disch, Dann, Le Guin, Dorman, Bishop and Brian Aldiss.

In the small press, Ackerson edited *Rocket Candy*, and three homespun magazines emerged that were devoted solely to speculative poetry: *Treaders of Starlight*, edited by Mark Rich, *Umbral*, edited by Steve Rasnic Tem, and my effort *Speculative Poetry Review* (SPR). Also, the scholarly review *Cthulhu Calls* ran an SF poetry contest and subsequently published many fine winners and runners-up. A significant number of poets surfaced in these publications who devoted most of their writing—at least for a time—to speculative poetry, including influential figures like Bruce Boston, Kathryn Rantala (K.E. Roney), Steve Sneyd, Gene van Troyer, David Lunde, Peter Dillingham, and Andrew Joron.

Suzette Haden Elgin must have sensed the oncoming wave as it crested, for she instituted the Science Fiction Poetry Association, its regular newsletter *Star*Line*, and the Rhysling Awards in 1978. She unified a movement before it hit the docks and rocked the boats in the Eighties, and she offered us the Rhyslings as a method of assessing not only the best the field had to offer, but the direction the field was taking.

**The Rhyslings Cometh**

Andrew Joron published two of his three Rhysling-winning poems in the Seventies (winners in 1978 and 1980), and I consider him a pure product of the movement. With little publishing experience behind him, he exploded from the gates, and his seemingly irreconcilable blend of surreal intent and hard science content is still unique to the field. In 1980's "The Sonic Flowerfall of Primes" (*New Worlds #216*), Joron tells a story without employing a conscious narrative thread, one that evokes two massive, sentient, orbiting satellites whose tragic tale of love is witnessed from below, like a great all-consuming soap opera, by residents of the failing civilization they oversee.

> Athwart the dead audience: a nightside lit with cities
> Zapping with bluest energy
> Binary citizenries, one- and zero-numbered
> Where *whose eternal cameras* scan
> The test patterns of our social constants

Gene Wolfe's 1978 experiment "The Computer Iterates the Greater Trumps" (*SPR #2*) runs backwards through its stanzas, and achieves prognostication in the exact manner its title implies, with an error message for an ending.

> Trump (0)
> *******Fool*******
> errorerrorerrorerror
> 23232323232323232323

In contrast to the surreal and experimental, Sonya Dorman's 1978 "The Corruption of Metals" (*2076*, Pyramid Books) offers pithy free verse.

> miles of glittering
> whales    unbuckled bellies
>         junked space ships
>         lie across hills

And from 1979, Michael Bishop recasts the 17th-century rhymes of Andrew Marvell into a poetic letter "For the Lady of a Physicist" from a love-struck black hole (*Black Holes,* Ace Books).

> Therefore, I have become for her
> A dark, entropic murderer,
> Whose chiefest virtue is his pull.
> Then, while my strength is at its full,
> Let me draw her to my embrace,
> Collapse her will and show my face.

From the initial years onward, the Rhyslings favor no poetic form or style, and the winners originate from books and publications with varied circulations.

**Trends: the Eighties and Beyond**

A new decade brought change. The big SF magazines seemed to use poems in every issue, often more than one. A fresh crop of small poetry magazines like *Velocities, Uranus, Ice River, Dreams and Nightmares*, and *The Magazine of Speculative Poetry* focused wholly on speculative work. Steve Tem brought out *The Umbral Anthology of Science Fiction Poetry* (Umbral Press, 1982), and I amassed *Burning With A Vision* (Owlswick Press, 1984) as a mix of science and SF works (both reprinted "The Head-Rape," it should be noted). *Science* magazine, the publisher of three pure science Rhysling winners from 1983-85, issued the landmark science poetry anthology *Songs From Unsung Worlds,* edited by Bonnie Gordon. Ocean View Books developed a line of speculative poetry projects that included doubled author collections, much like Ace doubles, plus a box set of *Velocities* and a major anthology in 1989 titled *Poly: New Speculative Writing,* edited by press founder Lee Ballentine.

I remember annual pilgrimages to San Francisco when Andy Joron and Bruce Boston would tour me through the bookstores, and there were always new and surprizing materials on the stands like *Kayak* and *Grimoire*, as well as overlooked volumes to probe like Richard Grossinger's *Mars: A Science Fiction Vision* (Io Books, 1971) or Ray DiZazzo's *Clovin's Head* (Red Hill Press, 1976). The discussion inevitably circled back to *Holding Your Eight Hands* and the association.

SF poetry had finally reached a larger arena.

As the Rhysling Awards matured throughout the Eighties and

Nineties, they maintained an eclecticism consistent with this growth. In 1983 another true surreal work, Adam Cornford's lengthy "Your Time and You", won beside a true science poem from a well-known scientist, "In Computers" by Alan Lightman. In 1984 established forms reigned with 3-time-winner Joe Haldeman's paired sestinas winning the long poem category and Helen Erhlich's paired sonnets winning the short, yet in 1985 a pair of free verse poems took the long and short honors, one a letter on astronomy in poetry form by Siv Cedering and one a cautionary tale on star travel by 7-time-winner Bruce Boston, fully-realized in just seven couplets.

> if you've kissed the burning eyelids
> of god and seized upon the moon's
>
> reflection, disjointed and backwards,
> in the choppy ink of some alien sea,
>
> then you know how sleek and fleshy,
> how treacherous, the stars can become.

Jump to 2003 and we still see a variety of works in the winners' circle—an epic off-world science fantasy poem, a poem of horrific seduction, and one that offers light-hearted yet practical magic for gardeners.

This does not mean that other trends haven't coalesced during 27 years of the award. They have.

A fair appraisal of the sixty-three winners from 1978 to 2004 reveals a penchant for storytelling. A majority of the poems narrate a story; and while this may also be true in the mainstream of poetry, the mainstream eschews poems shaped by fictitious characters and events and favors confessional poems (about the poet and their life). From the unnamed protagonist in Duane Ackerson's 1978 winner "The Starman" to Octavia in the 2004 winner "Octavia is Lost in the Hall of Masks" by Theodora Goss, Rhysling poets lean the other way. The exceptions to this would be my 1994 confessional poem "Salinity," as well as Haldeman's "January Fires" and Boston's "My Wife Returns As She Would Have It," both from 2001. Otherwise, the trend stands.

Another observation . . . excepting Le Guin's "The Well of Baln" from 1982, the first 10 years of association voting were dominated by science fiction and pure science works, but starting with late Eighties Rhysling picks like "Daedalus" by 4-time-winner W. Gregory Stewart (1987) and "White Trains" by Lucius Shepard (1988), fantasy and horror poems have displayed equal levels of popularity. I'd say this parallels the historical trends in fantastic fiction since the mid-Eighties, and little else can be concluded, save that the concerns of fiction writing again appear to have an affect on SF/speculative poetry.

## Defining Tomorrow

Our poetry readers still prefer visionary imagery with the emotional zip that only SF poets can deliver, a combination that Andrew Joron calls poetic "velocity," and they shy away from nothing. Especially tough questions.

Is science fiction poetry necessarily dependent on telling a story, dependent on the fiction side of its equation? Is science fiction poetry different because of this? The trends I have isolated seem to indicate that the field remains unsure whether its identity hinges on its poetics or on its fantastical subject matter. Does this truly amount to a crisis? Unlikely. I overstated that at first to get your attention. I'd argue that it's healthy for SF/speculative poets to re-evaluate what they are writing and where they are going.

In a sense, *The Alchemy of Stars* forces the issue. You hold a volume of seminal poetry by a who's who in the field, and that should be enough to engage you, to cause you to re-think what you knew or thought you knew about SF poetry. It truly engages me.

If you haven't read poetry like this before, I envy you . . . you're choosing from the gourmet menu for your first taste.

### Rhysling Synchronicites

**Back-to-back winning poets:** Duane Ackerson, 1978-79; Bruce Boston, 1988-89; Laurel Winter, 1998-99.

**1983-85:** Each year featured a winner from *Science* magazine.

**1984:** Both winners feature paired poems, and both are in strict poetry forms, the sestina and the sonnet.

**1996:** The winning poets became husband and wife five years later.

**1997:** Both winners are dedicated to other science fiction writers.

**2001:** Both winners are confessional poems about the specific lives of the poets.

**2002:** Both winners are dialectic poems about the general condition of mankind.

*The Rhysling Winners*

## GENE WOLFE

# *The Computer Iterates the Greater Trumps*

*DEMENSION* Trumps (21)
Do 1969 1 = 1,22
N = 22-1
Trump (N)
Trump (21)
*The Universe* includes by definition all,
That Man has seen since the great fall.
God's calling card this, upon our silver Disch,
On what table? In what house? In what hall?
Trump (20)
*The L6a6s6t Judgement*, and my creed betrays,
Unlearnt foreknowledge of those coming days.
The angels come to smite the sea and land,
The anti-Christ for us—and slays.
Trump (19)
*The Sun* the dancing children love,
Casts down this radiance from above.
Fusion, fission, no remission;
So small a house, so large a stove.
Trump (18)
*The Moon*, stillborn sister of our Earth Pale
Faced observes the living birth.
Soon, soon, the sister's children come,
to plow and plant that stoney turf.
Trump (17)
*The Star*, sky-ruler by default,
Pours out two waters: fresh, and salt.
Naked, bare breasted girl, and (whisper)
Magna Mater of the Old Cult.
Trump (16)
*The Falling Tower* smote by God,
Thunders in ruins to the sod.
Master, it needs no wit to read this card.
Master, you must wait his rod.
Trump (15)
*The Devil* straddles his searing throne,
With power in his hands alone!

He says,
We have been shown; we have been shown; we have been shown.
Trump (14)
*Death* in this deck's no gibb'ring shade;
But naked peasant with a blade;
Think on that, thou unfought people! and,
Remember whence these cards were made.
Trump (13)
*The Hanged Man* hangs by his feet,
Knew you that? His face, so sweet,
Almost a boy's.
He hangs to bleed. Who waits to eat?
Trump (12)
*The Wheel of Fortune*; cause and effect;
God will save his own elect;
The wheel turns until it stops—
The bitch within runs 'til she drops.
Trump (11)
Sworded *Justice* weighs us men,
Then, sordid weighs us up again.
Were't not more justice just to slay?
Slaying sans guilt to slay again?
Trump (10)
*Fortitude* with hands like laws,
Clamps shut the writhing lion's jaw;
Ignoring his beseeching eye.
Ignoring his imploring paws.
Trump (9)
Taking two hands in the Tarot game,
*Temperance*, with *Time* her other name.
Pouring light into a golden cup.
Watering our wine. Drowning our fame.
Trump (8)
*The Hermit* with his lamp and staff,
Treads all alone his lonely path.
He who hath no one,
Know you who he hath?
Trump (7)
*The Lovers* mean birth as well as lust,
Read ye that riddle as ye must;
Men from semen, O ye people!
Dust from dust from dust from dust.
Trump (6)

*The Chariot's* a Gypsie car,
And we the happy drivers are,
with whip and reins and endless pains,
So far, so far, so far.
Trump (5)
*The Emperor* for worldly power,
To shake and scream a fleeting hour;
To this a bribe, to that a bullet—
Remember, Mater, the *Falling Tower*?
Trump (4)
*The Hierophant*, *The Pope*, *The Priest*;
Today we fast, tomorrow feast.
The bridegroom was with us yesterday;
*The Hierophant* remains, at least.
Trump (3)
*The Lady Hierophant*, good *Pope Joan*,
Who will not let the truth alone;
A scholar killed her yestereve,
Today she's sidling towards the throne.
Trump (2)
*The Empress, Nature*, loving and cruel,
Grim mistress of the one hard school,
Mistress of microbes,
Breaking each tool.
Trump (1)
*The Juggler* points both down and up, in mastery of confusion;
First in all the deck stands he, creator of illusion.
Sword, coin, and cup before him lie,
And on his face derision.
Trump (0)
******FOOL******
errorerrorerrorerror
23232323232323232323

1969

## Duane Ackerson

### *The Starman*

When he left the earth was green,
the children loose in the fields
like dandelion spores.

When he returned it was green,
the children were still running.
He tried to catch them,
but they whispered
through his fingers like ghosts.

There were a few new machines:
they tried to comfort him.
One vacuumed the wrinkles
from his face,
lifted them off as easily as spiders;
another breathed a summer sun
into his head,
shook the cobwebs loose.
But he couldn't walk in a meadow
holding a machine by the hand;
he couldn't teach it to fly a kite.
The robots were elsewhere, anyway,
flying spaceships,
mining the moons of Jupiter,
miming geishas in the pleasure domes
of Pasha IV.
The children smelled the years in him;
women shunned him like Old Man Time.

He rested in the field,
holding a dandelion,
thinking of the sun
that once sat on its stalk.
Of the sun he'd traded for the moon,
the moon he'd traded for the stars.

Exhaling, he scattered its silver head.

## Sonya Dorman

### *Corruption of Metals*

miles of glittering
whales    unbuckled bellies
    junked space ships
    lie across hills

    berry bushes twiggle
    along titanium espaliers

the winter solstice lies down
on padded couches    frost enters
    the solar vanes
    with white tentacles

the cameras dream of space
    the way captains
    in black silence
once thought of earth

## Andrew Joron

### *Asleep in the Arms of Mother Night*

One millennium more
An old woman walking in the snow
Follows the light at the center of the Earth
Should she find it, we shall wake
We travelers in sleep; Earth's children
Each walking alone in our own forest of stars

With a Moon like the soul of winter ascending
To the home of all last things
Here is nothing that is complete
These white nights are still as all the forests forgotten
All lost in her head, as her children are lost
In the forests, far in the star-fields
Where oldening clouds, and sacral hours
Later, on thoughts long journey to some earthly center
She steps down into the ancient stone cists

And here, like a hundred Decembers
Of this old world's last century
In silent apocalypse
Does the snow on our tools' tombs descend

A silence whose center is nowhere—whose softest
Circumference seems infinite as our failing
To say what we know in this stillness is true
Of Time, wearing the faces of all other children
Of a light held in the dark Earth's hand

To the cislunar spaces our words are spoken
Signals transmitted in the tides and sky
Slow as geologic ages
Our dreams entropic heat and light
Our lives are the data
Trapped in a wave-train of necessity and nothingness
The messages of that mother
Who is the soul of Earth, and mortal

Who delivers at dawning to the dark man's hand
All things in her old cloud sack; a whole world's sleeping
Phosphorescent infants bundled in black
And all things tooled finely, all things learned
Ask something of forever
But tonight she is their answerer in body: Time's whore
Dancing endlessly his rounds
Her children shall some day become him

MICHAEL BISHOP

## *For the Lady of a Physicist*

*after Andrew Marvell*

Although Bekenstein's hypothesis that black holes have a finite entropy requires for its consistency that black holes should radiate thermally, at first it seems a complete miracle that the detailed quantum-mechanical calculations of particle creation should give rise to emission with a thermal spectrum. The explanation is that the emitted particles tunnel out of the black hole from a region of which an external observer has no knowledge other than its mass, angular momentum and electric charge. This means that all combinations or configurations of emitted particles that have the same energy, angular momentum and electric charge are equally probable. Indeed, it is possible that the black hole could emit a television set or the works of Proust in 10 leather-bound volumes.

— Stephen Hawking

If I with her could only join
In rapturous dance, loin to loin,
Deep space itself would soon discern
Galactic rhythm in our burn.
Our bodies stars, our debts all void,
Then would we waltz and, thus employed,
Inflate with megacosmic thrust
Through night and death and sifting dust.
Godlike lovers, we would hang
Beyond the cosmos whose Big Bang,
All the mad millennia past,
Was but a popgun to our slow blast.
And as we reeled with raw élan,
Pulsing plasma in vast pavane,
We would shame the Pleiades,
Relume the Magellanic Seas,
Deliver all our Milky Way,
Ionic flux too fierce to stay,
In supernova, and so rehearse
Our own expanding universe.
But my small body is no star,
Albeit something similar:

A blind pool vacuuming into it
All the lambency it's not fit
To redirect and render rife.
The woman I would take to wife
Sees only blackness in my eyes,
Rapacious ebon, hungry skies,
An O-gape gravid with desire
To aggrandize itself in fire;
And so her light sweeps down the hole
That is the maelstrom of my soul.
  Therefore, I have become for her
A dark, entropic murderer,
Whose chiefest virtue is his pull.
Then, while my strength is at its full,
Let me draw her to my embrace,
Collapse her will and show my face.
With her my Beatrician guide,
We'd tunnel with the thermal tide
Into the arms of Betelgeuse—
With Quasar sets and Marcel Proust
Emergent with us, glory-bound,
Detritus of God's Lost & Found.
Thus, though we cannot create light
from love, yet we will vanquish night.

## Duane Ackerson

### *Fatalities*

Every time the clock strikes another hour, it falls over, dead, on the mantel. The clock strikes quite a few. Soon the mantel is littered with hours. Some are blue, some, gray, some, black, some, yellow; it begins to look like someone has been chopping up a rainbow for kindling and then, leaving the kindling by the clock instead of the fire. A natural mistake, knowing the clock's appetite for everything. Without historians to sort things out as they pass single file, a whole Roman Empire might rush through the mouth of the clock in a single afternoon, like newspapers leaping in the mouth of a fire.

## Steve Eng

### *Storybooks and Treasure Maps*

The kings and their crusaders are forgotten,
No one reads about them any more,
The flowers that the princess held are rotten,
Crushed beneath her slipper on the floor.

The chivalry of knights-in-armour's ended,
Fading like a fable into time,
The castle and the walls are undefended,
Empty like an ancient nursery rhyme.

But you and I must fight, and not surrender
All the dreams of yesterday we knew;
The grown-ups better listen and remember
Storybooks and treasure maps are true.

The demons and the dragons are all sleeping,
The giant's resting quiet in his bed,
The witches and the wizards now are keeping
Company with dreams that all are dead.

You and I must stand against tomorrow,
Fighting off the fear of growing old,
Dreams aren't something you can steal or borrow,
You don't beg them back once they've been sold.

But you and I must fight, and not surrender
All the dreams of yesterday we knew;
The grown-ups better listen and remember
Storybooks and treasure maps are true.

## Andrew Joron

### *The Sonic Flowerfall of Primes*

We welcome these cool auspicious hours
A red dusk on the radar promenades
A muted gong: and like ghosts accusing us
This *agape*'s guests appear
Surely to ascend again
Their angry forum—O golden solons
From a metal-poor Utopia
We shall dismantle them anon

It is a brittled language they must speak
For our attention: fingering
Some little machine-pressed rose of Number in their hope

We raise up columns of soft light
Far out of these dust-white airs: undinal
A radio sings, but the signal is failing
Its static sadly
Echoes not a datum across the courtyard
Our precessing singer's artificial star portends 0 – 0 – 0
He'll see this dusk
A blood-edged knife as it falls from the hand

Of our thin white mistress Moon
He sees too our mortal remains: now our metal habitations
Stained cirrus & the heart of continents stilled
We absolve ourselves there & above, wash in the Absolute
Most through his absolutions, his blood-soluble
Emotions
. . . Piquant telemetries, per hour passed downlink, into rooms
Where no shadow is

Fly in electra, he
Suspends our veiled supper of the Masses
So that even as we view him now, orbiting nightward
A blue-green blip on verdigris'd scanners
One favored dwarf or fool; the player on his oud
Must pluck blossoms of this Sun-heightened music
Holy notes to nerve the optick stem

His fingers light-spun on the frets
A spine that to our blood-beat banks
Must speed wishes & electric measures

The signal fades & our thoughts turn out of color
Other words are activated: revenants of his twenty-hundredth
Revolution—songs, devoted to his female double
Whom we'd developed as the back-up unit: she shared
His programming, smiled or sorrowed / and grew ill

On-line, the thread of her own breath broken
While he played one night upon his oud
A gold untuned Eternal thread

Those noon orbits he sang for one who sat alone
Her head bent to the stone
Never to know him except as herself
And herself as the embodiment of a star-blind purpose
Separate as two monads, each felt the other's suffering
Both remained distrustful of their symmetried desires
His studied fingers had never touched that throat
To strum glad cry, the gong resounding in her eye

Still she came to him in dreams, as our neural s(t)imulating shows
Still pained with the magneto-prints of their closed-loop identical
Design, they made love (or so each of them supposed)
. . . A face turned to the wall, fearsome, yet triumphantly
Aflame: her smoky skin, the black hair curled
Upon her neck like ciphers
And his naked torso arcing out the window, Heaven's inverse
All below, in the dark brass bowl of Sahara dayside

Then their bodies were wasted, cells and fibers
Accelerated, to meet our stony stillness
Toward the light's abandoned dwellings
Those energy-sinks where a gelid aether drips
And our voice dies in its echo
But his thoughts of her were subtler by their weakness
Palely pictured
Like the meaningless calligraphies
Arising from a blown-out candle

Beyond the Moon all motion
Must be uniform and circular as sleep / There

Stands a hermaphrodite of whom it is impossible to speak

The distance of an Absolute love is hers
She'll not acknowledge the votive ranks of technicians below
Hungering sheep on that once-green hill

When their missile hangars open rusty eyelids
Down a pew-narrow dull perspective; he hears dust
Delayed booms in midnight air
When, heart-frozen, he speaks to her from his steady star—we obey

As zeniths late the fuller Artemis, we have only
The safekeeping of being: a sere system, the steering of these cogs & wheels
To follow his or her thought's helpless longitudes
And in flights of neutralized Inertial joy
Our flame-winged barques roll out and Out

Athwart the dead audience: a nightside lit with cities
Zapping with bluest energy
Binary citizenries, one- and zero-numbered
Where *whose eternal cameras* scan
The test patterns of our social constants

Beyond the mile-high buildings
Earth & sky are
Rising discs, but he chords them gone
Abstract icons call them back again
As useful (shimmering
Heat-hymns across the civilized moraine)

We applaud: the player shall timely please
Us moving glacial megadromes
He alone in his cat-carved spacecraft *Thoth*
Lets his oud decrease the fire-line of day

The inanimate horizon acts against him
Finally: vagaries of wind & water, after the Sun goes
Erect cloud-cities / vast
in their changing, gas Urs and Chicagos
That cannot mean to mock our dying
Intentions—though farther off we hear
Our heartbeat's brief god-protecting thunder
Its one cause, those ionized highways on which no courier rides

Today's dreaming of the landscape is done
That set free the citizenries into our fine-tooled deserts
And did not let the six-armed towers collapse
& saw winter forests blow away like seeds
Who else looks down on the glittering wastes
Where we were sovereign?
Who knows better the rubble left behind
By these technologic glaciers

The human center all in one head, his despair
Is our consent: fixed here & efficient
His one response to the manufacture of her Miracles
A thing, reclining to this feast of fools
We shall not cease to measure

## Robert Frazier

### *Encased in the Amber of Eternity*

From the vantage of my cabin porch,
I see the flames as waves lap along the coast,
and the Torchships fall like comets,
dancing a St. Vitus dance;
fireflies hovering over the pyre of Portland.
Every major city on the continent has crumbled,
sticks of charcoal and lumps of eraser gum.
Power plants are melted into slag,
paint squeezed from the tube.
Telephone poles stand uselessly in bunches,
brushes shorn of their bristles.
The art of devastation is as subtle as the Florentine flood.
In the countryside the vineyards of the living go on,
but the wine is flat.
Blank televisions stare back at the blank faces,
a poetry of truly blank verse.
Yet here in my mountain retreat only time has changed,
crystallized into honey,
as I stock up for a long winter.
Its length stretches out before me
like the glow of an eternal sunset
spread out over the dark silhouettes of Oregon pine.
The snows are coming;
white pages of a new history
falling upon itself.

## Peter Payack

# *The Migration of Darkness*

Each evening, shortly after sunset,
darkness covers the land.
    Having mystified thinkers for millennia,
    the mechanism for this occurrence
    has now been identified: migration.
Darkness, it has been found, is composed
of an almost infinite number of particles,
which roost and reproduce up north
where they have fewer natural enemies:
    Forest fires, lampposts, lasers, blazing sunlight,
    torches, candles, lighthouses, limelight, and electricity
    are relatively rare in the polar regions.
These lightweight bits of darkness
flock together and fly south each evening
to more fertile land in a never-ending search
for an abundant food supply.
With the coming of the rising sun,
they return to their northern nesting grounds.
However, not all specks of darkness migrate.
Some that are less adventurous
    or downright lazy
choose to stay behind.
These covey together, in varying numbers,
seeking shelter from the strong sunlight
    by gathering under leafy trees, behind
    large rocks, and underneath umbrellas;
    hiding in alleys, between parked cars,
    in caves, and inside empty pockets.
These clusters are perceived by us as shadows.
They have a somewhat shorter life span
than those which migrate.

## Ken Duffin

### *Meeting Place*

Not in my lifetime, nor that of my sun;
but beyond the final collapse when
the last static ashes and
clinkered proteins bleed
slowly, from the mircocracks of the next
cosmic egg—then
and there will spin
the tiny helix, eternally recurring,
lapped by pale and teeming future seas.

Perhaps we'll meet?
Say yes;
say . . . an eon from now,
beside the gently sloping banks
of the gene pool. Come
as you were,
and I'll bring the wine.

URSULA K. LE GUIN

# *The Well of Baln*

1. *Count Baln*

I am a nobleman of vast estate,
girthed like an oak tree.
I own the oldest forests, oak and ash,
and the mountain lakes
where swans in autumn beat the wind to storm
unseen by other hunters. I am heir
to the house of seven hundred rooms,
its cornerstone the Standing Stone of Baln.
My heart beats slow and sound as a great bell.
But in the center of my house and heart a hole
is round and blacker than my beaver hat
and deeper than mines, deeper than roots of rivers.
And all the leaves and diamonds and hounds
fall into it, the hours and eyes and words,
the closer that I clutch them sooner gone,
and disappear. I lean above the well.
I call and gaze. No star, no stir.
Dry it goes down, dark and dry.
No rope, no bucket. No echo of my voice
or any voice. The hollowness
and the long dark stone way down.

I have let my candle fall into the well.
I have fired my hunting rifle into it.

Nothing shone or stirred or ever will.

What is the use of being a nobleman?

2. *Baln's Wife*

Why does he go there with his gun,
his old dog, or the sack
of rentgold from the eastern villages?
Why does he go into that room?
An empty cellar like a prison cell,

no door, no chair, no crucifix, no window,
bare. He goes in and he shuts the door.
I heard him speak aloud.

He came out without the gold.
I never saw the dog again.
He did not speak to me that day
nor look me in the eye that month.
In the dark early morning in our bed
I felt him shaking, but he did not speak.

If I knew what he feared!
I have searched that room on hands and knees
praying. There is nothing there.
Nothing stored; the bare floor;
nothing, nothing to fear.

3. *Baln's Daughter*

I have been down that well a hundred times.
I used to play with children with white hair
in one of the countries down inside the well
where all the rocks are glass.

If you turn to the side too soon
you get in the blind tunnels.
White birds, white bulls without eyes.
You have to go on down.

If you go down and down,
the person in the boat on the slow river
in the dark place said,
you will come clear out at last.

I crossed in the boat instead.
I paid the boatman with my father's gold;
he laughed and gave it back.

I like the country on the other side.

RAYMOND DIZAZZO

## *On the Speed of Sight*

Assume

that being human
we are much too fast
for the sight of plants

that flowers see
at the speed of blooming

grass in movements
of an inch per week

and snails are—
even to the fastest roses—
scarcely visible shots of light.

Sequoia then   and oak
see the slowest   watching
as the granite slopes

grow like teeth
and the constellations

lose their form.

## Adam Cornford

# *Your Time and You*
### A Neoprole's Dating Guide

*Since the writer has no means to escape, we want him to tightly embrace his time; it is his unique chance . . .*
— J.P. Sartre, 1945

Respond to your time's advances
all that flash
the zoom lens admiring you from a balcony
the bouquets of subway lines and low-cost flights
the invitations with Your Name Here
Accept a date

Out on the town with your time
give it a chance to show off
story after story blooming across its windows
spun-sugar wages
tall crystals oozing with power
Ooh as it flexes its lights and leans over you
Go home with it

Alone together
let its neoprene lips part gently against yours
its tongue slide buzzing along your gums
Ignore the faint aftertaste
scurvy and gun-oil
chlorine and Sahara and screams
Put your arms round it

Your time is a fast worker you should be too
talk with your fingertips
touch all the right keys and switches
feed it the hot numbers starting with you
the little pink secrets
Go through the motions until you sparkle with sweat
Undo its bracelet of extinct species
Whisper *yes*

Let its padded clamps rotate you
into position
its arms swivel down and move over you
sequence of sixty separate operations
Gaze up at your time
and smile
as your smile is replicated in mosaic flickers
your heat trace wriggles like a solar flare
Ignore the faint after-image
withered silk seizures
darkness blinking inside a vacuum flash
Whisper *please*

Let it part your thighs
with just enough of a struggle
the injector is pale and soft not
the stainless probe you expected
Caress it help it slide in move with it squeeze it
Whisper *now*

Writhe as its data pulse deep into you
sticky strings of hunger and skill
waste and speed and connections   its whole share
of future
Now feel the change
come over you   your body taper and streamline
your eyes become wet multiple rubies
your jaws segment and harden into a complex tool
razors sprout under your forearms
your millions of eggs flare like ether
already singing
children who won't need
to be what you are
Listen
Whisper *my turn*

Embrace your time tightly
before it can stagger away to new conquests
bite off its head

ALAN P. LIGHTMAN

## *In Computers*

In the magnets of computers will
  be stored

Blend of sunset over wheat
  fields.
Low thunder of gazelle.
Light, sweet wind on high
  ground.
Vacuum stillness spreading from
  a thick snowfall.

Men will sit in rooms
upon the smooth, scrubbed earth
or stand in tunnels on the moon
and instruct themselves in how it
  was.
Nothing will be lost.
Nothing will be lost.

Joe Haldeman

# *Saul's Death*

**Two Sestinas**

1.

I used to be a monk, but gave it over
before books and prayer and studies cooled my blood,
and joined with Richard as a mercenary soldier.
(No Richard that you've heard of; just
a man who'd bought a title for his name.)
And it was in his service I met Saul.

The first day of my service I liked Saul;
his easy humor quickly won me over.
He confided Saul was not his name;
he'd taken up another name for blood.
(As had I—my fighting name was just
A word we use at home for private soldier.)

I felt at home as mercenary soldier.
I liked the company of men like Saul.
(Though most of Richard's men were just
fighting for the bounty when it's over.)
I loved the clash of weapons, splashing blood—
I lived the meager promise of my name.

Saul promised that he'd tell me his real name
when he was through with playing as soldier.
(I said the same; we took an oath in blood.)
But I would never know him but as Saul;
he'd die before the long campaign was over,
dying for a cause that was not just.

Only fools require a cause that's just;
tools, and children out to make a name.
Now I've had sixty years to think it over
(sixty years of being no one's soldier),
sixty years since broadsword opened Saul
and splashed my body with his precious blood.

But damn! we lived for bodies and for blood.
The reek of dead men rotting, it was just
a sweet perfume for those like me and Saul.
(My peaceful language doesn't have a name
for lewd delight in going off to soldier.)
It hurts my heart sometimes to know it's over.

My heart was hard as stone when it was over;
when finally I'd had my fill of blood
(and knew I was too old to be a soldier).
Nothing left for me to do but just
go back home and make myself a name
in ways of peace, forgetting war and Saul.

In ways of blood he made himself a name
(though he was just a mercenary soldier)—
I loved Saul before it all was over.

2.

A mercenary soldier has no future;
some say his way of life is hardly human.
But we did have our own small bloody world
(part aches and sores and wrappings soaking blood,
partly fear and glory grown familiar)
confined within a shiny fence of swords.

And how I learned to love to fence with swords!
Another world, my homely past and future—
once steel and eye and wrist became familiar
with each other, then that steel was almost human
(with an altogether human taste for blood).
I felt that sword and I could take the world.

I felt that Saul and I could take the world:
take the whole world hostage with our swords.
The bond we felt was stronger than mere blood
(though I can see with hindsight in the future
the bond we felt was something only human:
a need for love when death becomes familiar).

We were wizards, and death was our familiar;
our swords held all the magic in the world.
(Richard thought it almost wasn't human,

the speed with which we parried others' swords;
forever end another's petty future.)
Never scratched, though always steeped in blood.

Ambushed in a tavern, splashing ankle-deep in blood,
fighting back-to-back in ways familiar;
Saul slipped: lost his footing and our future.
Broad blade hammered down and sent him from this world.
In angry grief I killed that one, then all the other swords;
then locked the doors and murdered every human.

No choice, but to murder every human.
No one in that tavern was a stranger to blood.
(To those who live with pikes and slashing swords,
the inner parts of men become familiar.)
Saul's vitals looked like nothing in this world;
I had to kill them all to save my future.

Saul's vitals were not human, but familiar:
he never told me he was from another world:
I never told him I was from his future.

## HELEN EHRLICH

# *Two Sonnets*

**Love Song to Lucy**

Three million times your bones have swept around
The sun since last your warm brown foot walked here
Upon the veldt. The hills, the lake, were dear
To you, and morning flowers, and each sweet sound
Of bird. In meadows where you played were found
The beasts that fed and clothed you—life's career.
And so you lived, until one day in fear
You died, and never knew you would astound
A future race. What waves of time beyond
Your ken evolved your sires, and ours, and sent
You here to us upon this destined shore.
Where we, your seed, have found you and respond
In awe? You speak in tomes you never dreamt—
A parent-link to all that lies before.

**Lucy Answers**

Your turn will come—time upon time your bones
Will also sweep the sun, and from the clay
Strange creatures, on a far and stranger day,
With eye and hand the primal mind disowns,
Will find you there among the silvered stones—
Will lift you, brush the ancient years away
And sift your possibilities the way
You do with me, in hushed and puzzled tones.
Your seed will seek his sire in mark and line
And try to mold your face, as you mold mine.
Yet I knew not you'd issue forth from me,
Nor can you penetrate his mystery.
As silence holds all future time at bay,
So tides will turn and sweep him, too, away.

Siv Cedering

## *Letter from Caroline Herschel (1750-1848)*

*for Carol*

William is away, and I am minding
the heavens. I have discovered
eight new comets and three nebulae
never before seen by man,
and I am preparing an Index to
Flamsteed's observations, together with
a catalog of 560 stars omitted from
the British Catalogue, plus a list of errata
in that publication. William says

I have a way with numbers, so I handle
all the necessary reductions and
calculations. I also plan
every night's observation
schedule, for he says my intuition
helps me turn the telescope to discover
star cluster after star cluster.

I have helped him polish the mirrors
and lenses of our new telescope. It is
the largest in existence. Can you imagine
the thrill of turning it to some new
corner of the heavens to see
something never before seen
from earth? I actually like
that he is busy with the Royal Society
and his club, for when I finish my other work
I can spend all night sweeping
the heavens.

Sometimes when I am alone
in the dark, and the universe reveals yet
another secret, I say the names
of my long, lost sisters, forgotten
in the books that record
our science—

Aganice of Thessaly,
Hypatia,
Hildegard,
Catherina Hevelius
Maria Agnesi
—as if the stars themselves could

remember. Did you know that Hildegard
proposed a heliocentric universe
300 years before Copernicus? that she
wrote of universal gravitation 500 years
before Newton? But who would listen
to her? She was just a nun, a woman.
What is our age, if that age was dark?

As for my name, it will also be
forgotten, but I am not accused
of being a sorceress, like Aganice,
and the Christians do not threaten to
drag me to church, to murder me, like they did
Hypatia of Alexandria, the eloquent, young
woman who devised the instruments
used to accurately measure the position and
motion of

heavenly bodies.
However long we live, life is short, so I
work. And however important man becomes,
he is nothing compared to the stars.
There are secrets, dear sister, and it is
for us to reveal them. Your name, like mine,
is a song. Write soon,

Caroline

BRUCE BOSTON

## *For Spacers Snarled in the Hair of Comets*

If you've heard the stellar *vox humana*
the untuned ear takes for static,

if you've kissed the burning eyelids
of god and seized upon the moon's

reflection, disjointed and backwards,
in the choppy ink of some alien sea,

then you know how sleek and fleshy,
how treacherous, the stars can become.

While the universe falls with no boundary,
you and I sit in a cafe of a port city

on a planet whose name we've forgotten:
the vacuum is behind us and before us,

the spiced ale is cool and hallucinogenic.
Already the candle sparkles in our plates.

ANDREW JORON

## *Shipwrecked On Destiny Five*

Final communiqué: long wanderings
near the edge
Of the so-called "fractured" terrain
Where night is always falling

The largest of three suns
is tidally distorted
perpetually
Smeared above the south horizon
where the smallest
When eclipsed, burns a hole
Right through that giant's helium husk

None of us has spoken
much this morning
Since we sighted the Carven Cliffs
spectro-
Analyzed from orbit: walls of unnatural smoothness
reflective as water
But splashed at intervals
By a dark symbology

We buried Johnson there
Another case of petrification
—why
Should they all freeze
In that characteristic attitude
lacking instruments
It's sometimes difficult to tell
Death from life
there are nine of us left

Other phenomena, so far
Unreported: surely no miracles
Only a few
Sensory tricks—auguries in clear weather

the floating columns
Of indeterminate size
& substance—still pacing us in our travels
Like spirit-stanchions, an all-surveying
Ennead
the guardians
Of an abandoned world?—or the roving
Geometric shadows of our minds

An ocean clotted with pink algae
—their floral
Cycles of tiny outgassing
Fill the air
With the clamor of a million violins

weedy tissues
Woven into rocks—that seem to pulsate
Altering their hue
With the pattern of our voices

Mists of metallic particles
gathering in shapes
That tease & respond to the artistry of our despair

The whistling body of the atmosphere
Lowers upon us like a mountain
The very pores of skyflesh
appearing
In skeins & sinews of the airflow
Opening like graves of light around our heads

The chromium bones
of our landing craft become
A lost language of shiny objects
—the sacred gears
Of a god machine

& we must tread among these
warped totems
A crew of empty spacesuits
Mantled in corrosive
& caressing spume
Remote-controlled
By a host of artificial memories

motiveless, we must continue
Searching
For some piece of fallen science

ground down
To our knees by the heavy gravity
Until we assume
our final
& somehow mystical
Postures
forming a tradition
Of abstract sculpture
Scattered along a scarlet beach

## SUSAN PALWICK

# *The Neighbor's Wife*

It sprouts wings every few weeks
but as yet has flown no further
than the woodpile in the yard
where we found it six months ago.

Colin Wilcox thought it was his wife
returned as an angel. It still wore
its headset then, lying trapped
in a crushed metal basket; Colin freed it,

muttering something about harps and haloes,
and the rest of us stayed quiet. Colin carried it
into the house and for three weeks nursed it
in his bed, on the side unwarmed since Marella,

the old Marella, had her heart attack.
When it could walk on six legs Colin taught
it to fry bacon, weed the garden, milk
the goats, which cower at its touch.

"Reminding her what she forgot in Heaven,"
he tells us, but she has not remembered speech,
this new Marella who is purple and croaks
like bullfrogs on the hottest summer nights,

who surely came from somewhere, if not from God.
Lately it uses those stubby wings to carry
the heaviest logs from the woodpile. For Colin's sake
no one has tried to frighten it away.

W. GREGORY STEWART

## *Daedalus*

Father, if
you read this, I am dead,
a waxen wrack of flesh
and wing unfeathered. If
you read this,
you will know that I
have tried to touch the sun,
and you will know that in this
I have failed.

But do not grieve,
my father; do not grieve for me.
We spent our closest year
in grand and common dream.
We gathered quill
and plume in secret, sought
the dove for underwing
and hawk to wrap the winds about
our farthest reach.

Finch and elder,
eagle, too; the every barb
aligned, reset along its
shaft, then hidden, placed
by size and sort
behind the doors
behind the doors
(against the winds
and prying eyes).

And hives!
Oh, father, remember the hives?
Bees robbed for comb instead of
honey were no less angry for that
lesser theft.
I laid mud upon you and we laughed,
you as much of earth that day
as I (too briefly) have been of

the heavens.

Father, I pray
        you, shed no tears for me. Instead,
        a promise: to hold fast that dream.
        Know that it was arrogance—and accident—
but not the dream . . .
        my own damned fault perhaps, but it
        was not Apollo cast me down,
        and not the Fates:
they've never cared.

Keep your wings.
        This at the last—if only for
        my memory, cast not your wings away.
        Remember—I have seen the Heavens,
I have flown,
        and having flown would rather be
        as I am now than stricken down
        in dotage, weak and never having
known the sky.

## JONATHAN V. POST

### *Before the Big Bang*

**News from the Hubble Large Space Telescope**

The Astronomer was red eyed, pale,
his face was gray with stubble;
he was 13 on a sliding scale
of 1 to 10 in trouble.

"Is Physics just a fairy tale?"
he asked, and then began to wail,
"Why DID we seek the holy grail?
Why DID we launch the Hubble?

The launch was good (relax, exhale)
the data systems did not fail
we peered beyond the cosmic veil,
the anti-cosmic double

to back before the quarks prevail.
We digitized each dark detail
but it was all to no avail,
It burst our pretty bubble."

"WHAT did you see?" I asked "Before
Beginning Big Bang lights?"
(I reviews and interviews. I edits and I writes.)
"Before the start of Time, before the Universe's Birth,
What DID the Hubble show, ten billion years before the Earth?"
He told me. Now I writes no more.
I drinks a bit. I edits.
"Right before the Beginning," he said,
"is when THEY roll the credits!"

## JOHN CALVIN REZMERSKI

# *A Dream of Heredity*

I am walking around
with my son on my back
and his son sitting
on his son's back and
I get angry
because they
are getting
a free ride
and my
feet are
numb.
I look down at my feet and see
they are not moving—
I am sitting on my father's
shoulders and he is
sitting on his own
father's—we are
midway more or less
in a stack of men
that disappears way up
into clouds
like a tornado,
a tornado that spins
down to where
the stack rests
on the back of an ape who
is not too
bright but
has more
good will
and loyalty
than I have
ever felt
toward
him.

All around us, a mob of women locked arm in arm shout and argue about the whole stack of us, but they can come face to face only with the ape. Now and then they try to push us over, but whenever someone pushes at the front someone else pushes back from behind. We are a tower, impregnable and unyielding. They are a fierce and irresistible savanna. The air is full of the sound of explosions. The smell of powder is everywhere, and the astringent taste of stalemate. The battle is over. They cannot budge us and we cannot get off each others backs. We are all paralyzed because the ape can't move. I wake up saying, "Ease off, let the ape breathe. Let me

down."

LUCIUS SHEPARD

## *White Trains*

White trains with no tracks
have been appearing on the outskirts
of small anonymous towns,
picket fence towns in Ohio, say,
or Iowa, places rife with solid American values,
populated by men with ruddy faces and weak hearts,
and women whose thoughts slide
like swaths of gingham through their minds.
They materialize from vapor or a cloud,
glide soundlessly to a halt in some proximate meadow,
old-fashioned white trains with pot-bellied smokestacks,
their coaches adorned with filigrees of palest ivory,
packed with men in ice cream suits and bowlers,
and lovely dark-haired women in lace gowns.
The passengers disembark, form into rows,
facing one another as if preparing for a cotillion.
And the men undo their trouser buttons,
their erections springing forth like lean white twigs,
and they enter the embrace of the women,
who lift their skirts to enfold them,
hiding them completely, making it appear
that strange lacy cocoons have dropped from the sky
to tremble and whisper on the bright green grass.
And when at last the women let fall their skirts,
each of them bears a single speck of blood
at the corner of their perfect mouths.
As for the men, they have vanished
like snow on a summer's day.

I myself was witness to one such apparition
on the outskirts of Parma, New York,
home to the Castle Monosodium Glutamate Works,
a town whose more prominent sophisticates
often drive to Buffalo for the weekend.
I had just completed a thirty-day sentence
for sullying the bail bondsman's beautiful daughter
(They all said she was a good girl

but you could find her name on every bathroom wall
between Nisack and Mitswego),
and having no wish to extend my stay
I headed for the city limits.
It was early morning, the eastern sky
still streaked with pink, mist threading
the hedgerows, and upon a meadow bordering
three convenience stores and a laundromat,
I found a number of worthies gathered,
watching the arrival of a white train.
There was Ernest Cardwell, the minister
of the Church of the Absolute Solstice,
whose congregation alone of all the Empire State
has a written guarantee of salvation,
and there were a couple of cops big as bears
in blue suits, carrying standard issue golden guns,
and there was a group of scientists huddled
around the machines with which they were
attempting to measure the phenomenon,
and the mayor, too, was there, passing out
his card and declaring that he had no hand
in this unnatural business, and the scientists
were murmuring, and Cardwell was shouting
"Abomination," at the handsome men
and lovely women filing out of the coaches,
and as for me, well, thirty days and the memory
of the bail bondsman's beautiful daughter
had left me with a more pragmatic attitude,
and ignoring the scientists' cries of warning and
Cardwell's predictions of eternal hellfire,
the mayor's threats, and the cops' growling,
I went toward the nearest of the women
and gave her male partner a shove and was amazed
to see him vanish in a haze of sparkles
as if he had been made of something insubstantial
like Perrier or truth.

The woman's smile was cool and enigmatic
and as I unzipped, her gown enfolded me
in an aura of perfume and calm,
and through the lacework the sun acquired
a dim red value, and every sound was faraway,
and I could not feel the ground beneath my feet,

only the bright sensation of slipping inside her.
Her mouth was such a simple curve, so pure
a crimson, it looked to be a statement of principle,
and her dark brown eyes had no pupils.
Looking into them, I heard a sonorous music;
heavy German stuff, with lots of trumpet fanfares
and skirling crescendos, and the heaviness
of the music transfigured my thoughts,
so that it seemed what followed was a white act,
that I had become a magical beast with golden eyes,
coupling with an ephemera, a butterfly woman,
a creature of lace and heat and silky muscle . . .
though in retrospect I can say with assurance
that I've had better in my time.

I think I expected to vanish, to travel
on a white train through some egoless dimension,
taking the place of the poor soul I'd pushed aside,
(although it may be he never existed, that only
the women were real, or that from those blood drops
dark and solid as rubies at the corners of their mouths,
they bred new ranks of insubstantial partners),
but I only stood there jelly-kneed watching
the women board the train, still smiling.
The scientists surrounded me, asking questions,
offering great sums if I would allow them to do tests
and follow-ups to determine whether or not
I had contracted some sort of astral social disease,
and Cardwell was supplicating God to strike me down,
and the mayor was bawling at the cops to take me
in for questioning, but I was beyond the city limits
and they had no rights in the matter, and I walked
away from Parma, bearing signed contracts
from the scientists, and another presented me
by a publisher who, disguised as a tree stump,
had watched the entire proceeding, and now
owned the rights to the lie of my life story.
My future, it seemed, was assured.

White trains with no tracks
continue to appear on the outskirts
of small anonymous towns, places
whose reasons have dried up, towns

upon which dusk settles
like a statement of intrinsic greyness,
and some will tell you these trains
signal an Apocalyptic doom, and
others will say they are symptomatic
of mass hysteria, the reduction of culture
to a fearful and obscure whimsy, and
others yet will claim that the vanishing men
are emblematic of the realities of sexual politics
in this muddled, weak-muscled age.
But I believe they are expressions of a season
that occurs once every millennium or so,
a cosmic leap year, that they are merely
a kind of weather, as unimportant and unique
as a sun shower or a spell of warmth in mid-winter,
a brief white interruption of the ordinary
into which we may walk and emerge somewhat
refreshed, but nothing more.
I lecture frequently upon this subject
in towns such as Parma, towns whose lights
can be seen glittering in the dark folds of lost America
like formless scatters of stars, ruined constellations
whose mythic figure has abdicated to a better sky,
and my purpose is neither to illuminate nor confound,
but is rather to engage the interest of those women
whose touch is generally accompanied by
thirty days durance on cornbread and cold beans,
a sentence against which I have been immunized
by my elevated status, and perhaps my usage
of the experience is a measure of its truth,
or perhaps it is a measure of mine.

Whatever the case, white trains move silent as thought
through the empty fields, voyaging from nowhere
to nowhere, taking on no passengers, violating
no regulation other than the idea of order,
and once they have passed we shake our heads,
returning to the mild seasons of our lives,
and perhaps for a while we cling more avidly
to love and loves, realizing we inhabit a medium
of small magical transformations that like overcoats
can insulate us against the onset of heartbreak weather,
hoping at best to end in a thunder of agony

and prayer that will move us down through
archipelagoes of silver light to a morbid fairy tale
wherein we will labor like dwarves at the question
of forever, and listen to a grumbling static from above
that may or may not explain in some mystic tongue
the passage of white trains.

## BRUCE BOSTON

### *The Nightmare Collector*

Each night he calls you
for the leading role
in his gallery
of ancestral tableaus
which trails back
through the Pleistocene
to the red primeval.

From the endless slashes
in his voluminous greatcoat
you can feel the heat
of captured bodies
invade your rumpled bed
with delirium and fever;
you can smell a brassy
sediment of tears.

From the hollow blackness
of his flapping sleeves
you can hear the pulse
and thump of unborn shadows,
a dense hysteric fugue
winding up and down
the bones of your sleep.

The nightmare collector
waits on the landing
in the unlit hall
where the instruments
of ablation are arranged
on cold leather pallets,
where the dreamer's
balustrade of terror
rushes across landscapes
of a darkening retina,

where snakes coil about
your arms and ankles
and draw you down
bodily into a forest
of bloodstained hair.

## Suzette Haden Elgin

### *Rocky Road to Hoe*

The woman the stones spoke to ignored them;
knowing better. Fearing the thorazines.
Only after the rose quartz chunk said to her,
"Your little girl has fallen into the pool,"
and it was so,
did she accept the burdensome embedded knowledge.
Pointedly, gratingly,
she kept it to herself.
The stones had a dignity to their converse
appropriate to their formation,
the many-layered levels of meaning brought upward,
one at a time,
breaking through detritus,
not to be easily, ever, set aside.

She had the gravel in the driveway taken up,
and paved it over, grateful for concrete silence;
she removed the lovely slate from the side terrace
and laid down redwood over her husband's objections;
when driving through New Mexico and Arizona,
she stayed inside the car. At all times.
The day her daughters brought her a necklace of agates,
she carried it out to the garden and hung it high in a tree;
when that was not enough to hush its tinted voices,
she had her husband shut it away at the bank
in their safe deposit box. Saying,
"I can't leave something so precious just lying about."

But stones are everywhere.
Everyone else, being stone deaf, collects them.
Speaking to her from the fingers of friends and strangers alike,
they told her how it felt.
To be mined.

When the woman the stones spoke to died,
she left an enigma.
"Do not," she said in her will, "under any circumstances whatsoever,
bury me
beneath a stone."

BRUCE BOSTON

## *In the Darkened Hours*

So you are lost again
beneath the turning hub
of the fire flecked sky
and you call it a dream
as you wander the labyrinth
of streets and causeways,
past the shadow barges,
over the ice cloaked river,
down the rugged gullies
where you left behind
the satchels which hold
the weapons and the maps.

So you are lost again
where the night prevails
and you call it a dream
in the oldest city of all,
where the lighted towers
rise and fall like spokes
against the churning sky,
where the voices wail,
where you are engaged
in senseless conversation
with a host of familiar
strangers whose directions
lead you further astray.

So you must travel alone
without weapons or maps
to the house of your father,
past the wrought iron fences,
past the shores and lakes
of the naked arboretum,
past the fallen hillsides
and the deserted air field
where the burning engines
of destruction have fed.

So you climb the stairs
and discover the rooms
of your childhood have
blurred and shifted
like a moldering text,
door frames twisted
at elusive angles,
windows collapsed,
unbounded hallways
and shredded chambers
lifting off into space.

So you are lost again
in the night of the city.
So you must travel alone
to a house drawn from
your flesh and bones.
So you must do this
as the landscape changes.
So you must descend
the rugged gullies
while you forge
the faces of dead lovers.
So you must reassemble
the broken statuary
in your mother's garden
and leave your father's
books upon their shelves.
So you must speak with
the familiar strangers
who know your name.
So you must recite
from the annals
of your stillborn brother,
maniacal and devoted,
who takes your wrist
upon the stairs.

So you call it a dream:
this house you inhabit,
this city you traverse
with blind expectancy,
these faces you fashion

from the imperfect cloth
of memory transfigured,
these visions you conjure
in the darkened hours
with haunting replication.

# Winter Solstice, Camelot Station

## *John M. Ford*

Camelot is served
By a sixteen-track stub terminal done in High Gothick Style,
The tracks covered by a single great barrel-vaulted glass roof framed
upon iron,
At once looking back to the Romans and ahead to the Brunels.
Beneath its rotunda, just to the left of the ticket windows,
Is a mosaic floor depicting the Round Table
(Where all knights, regardless of their station of origin
Or class of accommodation, are equal),
And around it murals of knightly deeds in action
(Slaying dragons, righting wrongs, rescuing maidens tied to the tracks).
It is the only terminal, other than Gare d'Avalon in Paris,
To be hung with original tapestries,
And its lavatories rival those at Great Gate of Kiev Central.
During a peak season such as this, some eighty trains a day pass through,
Five times the frequency at the old Londinium Terminus,
Ten times the number the Druid towermen knew.
(The Official Court Christmas Card this year displays
A crisp black-and-white Charles Clegg photograph from the King's
own collection,
Showing a woad-blued hogger at the throttle of "Old XCVII,"
*The Fast Mail* overnight to Eboracum. Those were the days.)
The first of a line of wagons has arrived,
Spilling footmen and pages in Court livery,
And old thick Kay, stepping down from his Range Rover,
Tricked out in a bush coat from Swaine, Adeney, Brigg,
Leaning on his shooting stick as he marshalls his company,
Instructing the youngest how to behave in the station,
To help mature women that they may encounter,
Report pickpockets, gather up litter,
And of course no true Knight of the Table Round (even in training)
Would do a station porter out of Christmas tips.
He checks his list of arrival times, then his watch
(A moon-phase Breguet, gift from Merlin):
The seneschal is a practical man, who knows trains do run late,
And a stolid one, who sees no reason to be glad about it.
He dispatches pages to posts at the tracks,

Doling out pennies for platform tickets,
Then walks past the station buffet with a dyspeptic snort,
Goes into the bar, checks the time again, orders a pint.
The patrons half-turn—it's the fella from Camelot, innit?
And Kay chuckles soft to himself, and the Court buys a round.
He's barely halfway when a page tumbles in,
Seems the Knights are arriving, on time after all,
So he tips the glass back (people stare as he guzzles),
Then plonks it down hard with five quid for the barman,
And strides for the doorway (half Falstaff, half Hotspur)
To summon his liveried army of lads.

Bors arrives behind steam, riding the cab of a heavy Mikado.
He shakes the driver's hand, swings down from the footplate,
And is like a locomotive himself, his breath clouding white,
Dark oil sheen on his black iron mail,
Sword on his hip swinging like siderods at speed.
He stamps back to the baggage car, slams mailed fist on steel door
With a clang like jousters colliding.
The handler opens up and goes to rouse another knight.
Old Pellinore has been dozing with his back against a crate,
A cubical chain-bound thing with FRAGILE tags and air holes,
BEAST says the label, *Questing, 1* the bill of lading.
The porters look doubtful but ease the thing down.
It grumbles. It shifts. Someone shouts, and they drop it.
It cracks like an egg. There is nothing within.
Elayne embraces Bors on the platform, a pelican on a rock,
Silently they watch as Pelly shifts the splinters,
Supposing aloud that Gutman and Cairo have swindled him.

A high drivered engine in Northern Lines green
Draws in with a string of side-corridor coaches,
All honey-toned wood with stained glass on their windows.
Gareth steps down from a compartment, then Gaheris and Agravaine,
All warmly tucked up in Orkney sweaters;
Gawaine comes after in Shetland tweed.
Their Gladstones and steamers are neatly arranged.
With never a worry—their Mum *does* the packing.
A redcap brings forth a curious bundle, a rude shape in red paper—
The boys did that themselves, you see, and how does one wrap a
unicorn's head?
They bustle down the platform, past a chap all in green.
He hasn't the look of a trainman, but only Gawaine turns to look at

his eyes,
And sees written there *Sir, I shall speak with you later.*

Over on the first track, surrounded by reporters,
All glossy dark iron and brass-bound mystery,
The *Direct-Orient Express*, ferried in from Calais and Points East.
Palomides appears. Smelling of patchouli and Russian leather,
Dripping Soubranie ash on his astrakhan collar,
Worry darkening his dark face, though his damascene armor shows no
tarnish,
He pushes past the press like a broad-hulled icebreaker.
Flashbulbs pop. Heads turn. There's a woman in Chanel black,
A glint of diamonds, liquid movements, liquid eyes.
The newshawks converge, but suddenly there appears
A sharp young man in a crisp blue suit
From the Compagnie Internationale des Wagons-Lits,
That elegant, comfortable, decorous, close-mouthed firm;
He's good at his job, and they get not so much as a snapshot.
Tomorrow's editions will ask who she was, and whom with . . . .

Now here's a silver train, stainless steel, Vista-Domed,
White-lighted grails on the engine (running no extra sections)
The *Logres Limited*, extra fare, extra fine,
(Stops on signal at Carbonek to receive passengers only).
She glides to a Timken-borne halt (even her grease is clean),
Galahad already on the steps, flashing that winning smile,
Breeze mussing his golden hair, but not his Armani tailoring,
Just the sort of man you'd want finding your chalice.
He signs an autograph, he strikes a pose.
Someone says, loudly, "Gal! Who serves the Grail?"
He looks—no one he knows—and there's a silence,
A space in which he shifts like sun on water;
Look quick and you may see a different knight,
A knight who knows that meanings can be lies,
That things are done not knowing why they're done,
That bearings fail, and stainless steel corrodes.
A whistle blows. Snow shifts on the glass shed roof. That knight is gone.
This one remaining tosses his briefcase to one of Kay's pages,
And, golden, silken, careless, exits left.

Behind the carsheds, on the business car track, alongside the private
varnish
Of dukes and smallholders, Persian potentates and Cathay princes

(James J. Hill is here, invited to bid on a tunnel through the Pennines),
Waits a sleek car in royal blue, ex-B&O, its trucks and fittings chromed,
A black-gloved hand gripping its silver platform rail;
Mordred and his car are both upholstered in blue velvet and black leather.
He prefers to fly, but the weather was against it.
His DC-9, with its video system and Quotron and waterbed, sits
grounded at Gatwick.
The premature lines in his face are a map of a hostile country,
The redness in his eyes a reminder that hollyberries are poison.
He goes inside to put on a look acceptable for Christmas Court;
As he slams the door it rattles like strafing jets.

Outside the Station proper, in the snow,
On a through trick that's used for milk and mail,
A wheezing saddle-tanker stops for breath;
A way-freight mixed, eight freight cars and caboose,
Two great ugly men on the back platform, talking with a third on the
    ballast.
One, the conductor, parcels out the last of the coffee;
They drink. A joke about grails. They laugh.
When it's gone, the trainman pretends to kick the big hobo off,
But the farewell hug spoils the act.
Now two men stand on the dirty snow,
The conductor waves a lantern and the train grinds on.
The ugly men start walking, the new arrival behind.
Singing "Wenceslas" off-key till the other says stop.
There are two horses waiting for them. Rather plain horses,
Considering. The men mount up.
By the roundhouse, they pause,
And look at the locos, the water, the sand, and the coal,
They look for a long time at the turntable,
Until the one who is King says "It all seemed so simple, once,"
And the best knight in the world says "It is. We make it hard."
They ride on, toward Camelot by the service road.

The sun is winter-low. Kay's caravan is rolling.
He may not run a railroad, but he runs a tight ship;
By the time they unload in the Camelot courtyard,
The wassail will be hot and the goose will be crackling,
Banners snapping from the towers, fir logs on the fire, drawbridge down,
And all that sackbut and psaltery stuff.
Blanchefleur is taking the children caroling tonight,
Percivale will lose to Merlin at chess,

The young knights will dally and the damsels dally back,
The old knights will play poker at a smaller Table Round.
And at the great glass station, motion goes on,
The extras, the milk trains, the varnish, the limiteds,
The *Pindar of Wakefield*, the *Lady of the Lake*,
The *Broceliande Local*, the *Fast Flying Briton*,
The nerves of the Kingdom, the lines of exchange,
Running to schedule as the world ought,
Ticking like a hot-fired hand-stoked heart,
The metal expression of the breaking of boundaries,
The boilers that turn raw fire into power,
The driving rods that put the power to use,
The turning wheels that make all places equal,
The knowledge that the train may stop but the line goes on;
The train may stop
But the line goes on.

# Robert Frazier

## *Salinity*

Sweating in the full glare of August,
my father taught me a bittersweet truth
on a beach day, when he was restless
to be holding something
other than me—
a surf casting rod perhaps,
or the glow of health that eluded him and
corroded year by year like his station wagon
from halite poured on New England's icy roads.
He taught me that we preserved our heritage,
our only heritage really,
in the saltiness of our blood.
A striped bass can't live out of the sea,
he said, or in fresh water either.
Yet we carry our ocean with us from birth to beyond.
And as he cut short this speech,
fully knowing what carcinomas ate at him,
he let tears drop into the sea spraying on me.
Unmindful, I sucked the salt from my wrist.
Now it haunts my veins
those molecules of his within me,
that ocean within the head of a pin.
There whole ecologies of salinity,
of the evolution of things
once left unsaid,
await evaporation and condensation
and distillation.
Worlds reduced within worlds.
Lives within lives.
Yesterdays.

PATRICK MCKINNON

## *dear spacemen,*

i met you on tevee when i was a boy in the sixties.
back then you wore a lot of chrome-plated mylar
& had the heads of bugs.
have styles changed much for you?

i'm afraid i never should have sent this piece of earth;
there's disease down here
& disease can spread,
even to you, way out there in deep space.
i'm banking on its never arriving.
i know it's mad
but then again, you may have met my mother
somewhere in yr travels
on earth, before she died,
she was 4 foot 9 by 4 foot 9, big smile, drove a plymouth . . .

so, peace to you, spacemen.
we are all animals & rocks, humans, plants & gasses down here
& it's always a battle going on
over who's the strongest & smartest & best fucker.
the humans have big brains but don't use them very well.
i'm a human
& i'm worried
& just want you spacemen to know
about this planet we are beating up
same as we used to beat up jeff burdick and mat wenzel
& maurie pearlman in my old neighborhood.

this is a message in a bottle about humans
& may god bless whichever of you spacemen found it.
we have a joke here that goes:
there were three guys stranded on this desert island. one day a bottle floats to shore & they can't believe it. they uncork the bottle & out comes this genie, sez *hi boys, i'll grant you each one wish.* right away the first guy sez all he wants in the world is to go back to his wife & family & *blink* he's gone. so the second guy sez he too wants to go home & *blink* he's gone. this leaves the third guy, overcome w/grief because he did not have

a home or wife or family or friends anywhere on the planet. in despair at being left so abruptly alone, he blurts out, *damn i*

*sure wish those other two guys hadn't left me,* & *blink blink* there they are again, back on the desert island.

this is the sort of misfortune that's funny to us.

we continue building
this outrageous industrial complex
like mrs. winchester,
lone heiress to a brand
of rifles & guns we love so much.
thot if she never stopped
adding on to her house,
she'd live forever.
so for years the crews worked
round the clock
putting up wing after wing
& wall after wall &
staircase & hallways that lead to nowhere
& bathrooms & closets no one ever used
until finally the old girl died.
only five rooms were ever furnished.

but mrs. winchester wasn't the only one to die.
everyone who was alive when she was doing this
is certainly dead by now
& that's probably what makes us
so crazy here—
all the dying.

so spacemen take heed;
this may be ripe as comet juice
from a planet that's getting out of balance.
think of this as a snake
& don't open it.
don't let its fangs pierce yr skin.
don't let its tongue fondle & linger
inside yr pointy silver ears.
we like to kill things here.
it does something to us
like i guess we are always relieved it wasn't us who got killed.
in the end
we killed all of you

didn't we?

really tho, I'm sorry we constantly attacked yr ships
but it was just tevee
& i assume you got paid okay
& I imagine you got a little taste of our sex.
did the girls like yr shiny dicks?
did the boys like yr exotic vaginas?
did you ever have any babies from us?
what are their names?
do you have a name for us?
does it mean anything?
does it rhyme?

I want terribly to know what yr planet looks like. i
want to wander space like you do. i
want to stretch myself way out there
into some next place & stay for awhile.
on coming back i'd walk among the trees
& feel the distance,
feel the time it took
& live the rest of my life amazed.

o spacemen, i am groaning
against the limits of my human being,
leaning & breathing heavy as a man
who has grown too large for his only room.
my hands reach out
but I'm too far away for you to see.
please send me the secret
of yr silver suits
& the secret of your fishbowl helmets,
yr neon frisbee ship.
give me the secret of getting yrselves on tevee so much.

i'm a bartender down here
& i'm a writer too
tho not many people know about my writing.
i've been told to believe this is important
& somehow i've believed it.
maybe this letter will make me famous among *you*.
anyway, i pour drinks & people give me money to do it.
they wouldn't need me to pour drinks
if people didn't have to pay for them w/money.

is there money in space?

the way it works here is
they give me the money & i put it in the cash register.
i'd never trust the drinkers
to pour their own drinks
or put their own cash in the register
while i went downstairs to smoke some pot
& read a book for a few hours.

down here, doing something like that
would be called irresponsible
or crazy & they wouldn't give me any food.
they'd make me hitchhike the interstates as my home.
you can't trust anyone
so i pour all the drinks & take all the money
over & over again & sometimes i get drunk
because closing time comes faster that way
& i don't have to listen to the drinkers
telling me the same old crap one more time.
is pot legal in outer space?

if you raise your children well on our planet
they will grow up to be wiser than you are
& if you are afraid of that & raise them poorly
you'll be in the greater percentile.
you could listen to one of our creeks or rivers
for a hundred years & never
hear it all but we don't do much of that anymore.
most of us never get off the playground
chasing mirages of pleasure.
are yr people so incomplete?

i'm sorry to say we are very busy
climbing all over each other
like a mound of maggots in a pile of fresh dung.
we are so busy doing this,
we don't have time to come visit you
tho i realize it's our turn;
but believe me,
things haven't changed much since last you saw us.
we still want to kick yr asses all over space
& be in charge & take yr stuff & never give it back
& blow up a few stars along the way,

maybe even a sun
or some asteroids or a moon
or seal a black hole, collapse the entire universe
we're so mad & confused & spend our entire lives,
the lives we keep inside ourselves,
trying to get away from our idiot parents
or back to them & like I sed earlier,
my mother's dead;
have you seen her?
do you know anything about where the dead go,
if anywhere? please write.

do you have the mafia in space?
or communists or anarchists or ministers or liberals?
is there any corporate structure up there?
any bills to pay? any winter?
i heat w/electricity
& i see at night w/electricity
& use it to keep my food cold.
in fact, most of what goes on down here
happens somehow thru the use of electricity.
even our brains work on electromagnetic charges
& i've heard that electricity
may be what's causing all this recent cancer we've been having.
wouldn't that present a dilemma? i mean,
electricity is so useful & pretty
& profitable. & it paints over those unnervingly deep stars.
we are afraid of everything.

does our planet pulsate our fear into space
real loud like white noise cacophony?
do we radiate our darkness really far?
are we known about the universe
as that awful black sore
over in the milky way?
do you have any idea what we are supposed to be doing here?

are there cars on yr planet?
do you love them as much as we love ours?
are they more interesting & important to you
than yr children & yr grandchildren
& what sort of filth they are going to have to breathe?
we drive everywhere in our cars.
they make us fast as cheetahs

& stronger than grizzly bears & we don't like our bodies
so we've got the nice metal ones now.
& when we get tired of our particular model,
we can trade it in on something new & exciting.
& these cars are choking us to death
because our planet is just a large garage
w/the door forever closed
& so many of us putting keys into ignitions,
turning them on, relaxing in the bucket seats
w/the radio blaring songs that help us count backwards from ten.

o spacemen,
please come & get my family & me.
I don't know what we could do for you
except we are good at walking
& could go to yr store
& pick up whatever you might need for dinner.
andrea makes great bread & beautiful origami boxes
& really loves to garden. the children
have sweet music in their throats
& hearts full of trust & tremendous imaginations.
i blow the harmonica & see visions & tell stories.
i'm sure we'd have a good time.
we could take a picnic
to yr lakes & put our feet in yr water.
are yr lakes full of mercury?
do yr fish live or do they only die?
i hope you have eliminated malls on yr planet
& factories & suburbs & airports &
free enterprise. i hope yr top soil
won't be gone by 2025.

on the other hand,
i'm pretty sure
that by the time you get this letter,
there'll be no need
to reply.

sincerely,
pat mckinnon
planet earth
1989

## G. Sutton Breiding

### *Epitaph for Dreams*

There are the ancient hours
Of silence, dust and autumn sunlight.

There are the blue flowers of the empire,
Of grief and midnights made of endless cups

Of wine, and memory, and your face.
These are my fingers,

Lost in the lace of afternoons
When the aeons passed us by,

As we lolled in the coolest rooms
Of ivory, ice and sapphire.

This is my skull,
Behind the fretwork of flesh,

My fallen eyes gazing from an empty dynasty
Of darkness, still blind with visions

Of your radiant thighs half-wrapped
In silken coverlets,

Your breast sighing in pleasure
And in sorrow for the dying of our race,

We two, King and Queen,
Holding count amidst the shadows of the dead

Who lurk beyond the pillars
Of our guarded spells.

Morning glories hang from my ribs;
Tiny blue violets entwine my finger bones.

I watch the wine pass through me,
Into the silence, the dust, the autumn sunlight.

I wait now, in these ancient hours.

DAVID MEMMOTT

# *The Aging Cryonicist in the Arms of His Mistress Contemplates the Survival of the Species While the Phoenix is Consumed by Fire*

*". . . a 23-year-old ALCOR Suspension Member took his own life by a self-inflicted shotgun wound to the head . . . After the father was notified that his son was dead, he did not call ALCOR. Instead, he allowed his son to be autopsied without any intervention by ALCOR, made arrangements for pickup of his son's remains by a mortician who was a friend of the family, and had his son's remains cremated . . . For the first time in our history one of our Suspension Members has been lost beyond recall."*

— Mike Darwin, "Beyond Recall", *Cryonics*, June 1987

1.

They were already dead when we found them,
the trilobites, ammonoids and dinosaurs.
Their passing left no tracks of tears
on cheeks of activists stalled in the halls
of congress, awaiting the passing of bills.
Each shred of evidence recovered from thin layers of earth
recalls some episode, a piece of the great puzzle,
polarity shifts, climate changes, meteor impacts.
Five mass exterminations fracture the fossil record
roughly corresponding to five suns of Mayan myth,
four already plunged into darkness as even now the fifth fades.
The first world was the era of dark earth
and it died from oxygen, destroyed by wind.
The Sun of Air, the second world, sank under a fiery rain.
The Sun of the Rain of Fire drowned in a fourth world flood,
the flood waters then receded and the age of man was born.
Earth, air, fire, water, all balanced in man, the fifth sun,
symbolized by the equilateral cross with man at its juncture.
So fragile this thing called life,
depending on how you define it.

2.

They were already dead when I got there,
the ancient ones, sculptors of immense plazas,

engineers of great temples and pyramids,
astronomers extraordinaire.
I am humble as a Paiute in this low canyon
aware of my own smallness in the shadow of their works.
Carrying my heart in my hand, I mount the sacred stairway
and mark the movement of the Sun with their calendars.
What we bring back cannot compare to what was lost beyond
recall, looted legacies in a thousand private collections,
whole cultures scattered like burning embers
until every last spark dies in the wind.
Tenuous this thing called culture,
depending on who defines it.

3.
They were already dead when I got there;
all the saviors gone, their words written down in books.
I crack their bodies for light, but no light comes.
I try to strike the stars from cold stone
and alone put back into the heavens
what the measure of science brought down to earth
and placed fluttering so fragile in my fist.
I beat the shimmering dust of old myths from my palms,
ignite a fire with the friction of skin against skin.
So precious this thing called faith,
so dangerous when it closes a mind.
We kill the god in man.
Osiris, Orpheus, Quetzalcoatl, Christ!
Rise, my beautiful birds, rise from the ashes
with iridescent plumage of scarlet and gold.

4.
They were already dead when we got there,
the victims of the holocaust,
their ashes still warm
when we liberated the camps,
billowing black pillars of smoke from chimneys
still suspended over all of Europe
when we found the mountains of shoes and eyeglasses
that failed to help them run from or see
what was happening in those showers.
Bodies, all bone, stacked up for the crematoriums
and those we saved from the cool bureaucracy of death

were uncounted casualties wearing numbers on their flesh.
We kill the earth with our numbers.
Precarious this thing called man,
so dependent on who defines him.
Now man dreams his own successor—the machine—
and how, we wonder, will machine define itself?

**5.**

They were already dead when I got there,
the American mastodon,
Flightless ibis,
Carolina parakeet,
the Passenger pigeon,
Giant lemur,
the great auk.
The bleached bones of six million buffalo
animate my dreams and what remains of dying breeds
chide me as I have made no difference.
The California condor,
the Hawaiian o'o'-a'a' sings to himself,
for he is the last of his kind,
blue whale,
the Costa Rican spinner dolphin, human of the sea,
mountain gorilla,
snow leopard,
black rhinoceros,
the spotted owl.
They cry out from their homes, overrun by necessity,
and I stop my ears with music.
I go to work and sit entranced,
each day a day closer to joining the march to extinction.
We leave our record in wet cement,
a good impression of our mastering digits
mastering even our selves.

**6.**

He was already dead when they found him.
We cannot raise this Phoenix from ashes.
We will never know why he pulled the trigger
or whether he'd given up any thought of immortality
so chose to sabotage even a neurosuspension
by a shotgun wound to the head.

We would have saved him, you know, this once vital bird.
After a total blood washout and full body perfusion,
admittedly complicated by the headwound,
he would have been submerged in liquid nitrogen
and slowly cooled to -196 degrees centigrade
and placed in a cryocapsule to complete his first life cycle.
One day he would have been resurrected from this biostasis.
Nano-machines would have repaired the brain damage
and we could have asked him why?
Why did he give up so much so soon?
He would have had much time to think about it,
if, upon awakening, he could recall anything.
But now he is lost beyond recall.

7.

I was already dead when you found me, my dear,
dead but not buried, not lost beyond recall.
I was resurrected in your eyes, reborn in your arms—
so you see, I've already lived twice.
My name when formed on your lips is a lethal weapon;
it pierces the armor I'd so carefully forged.
You found a breach in my defenses and reached in
to heal me, your living touch better than any machine.
We must survive together.
What I want now is for both of us to live forever.
So please, my love, *sign here*.

## Joe Haldeman

### *Eighteen Years Old, October Eleventh*

Drunk for the first time in her life,
she tossed her head in a horsey laugh
and that new opal gift sailed off her sore earlobe,
in a graceful parabola,
pinged twice on the stone porch floor,
and rolled off to hide behind the rose bushes.

It gathered dust and silt for two centuries.
The mansion came down in a war.

For twelve thousand years
the opal hid in dark rubble, unmoving.
An arctic chill worked down through it, and deeper,
and glaciers pushed the rubble thousands of miles,
very fast, as opals measure time.

After millions of years (the Sun just measurably cooler)
a female felt the presence of a stone,
and waved away yards of snow and ice;
waved away dozens of yards
of frozen dirt and crushed rock,
and held, in what resembled a hand,
this bauble of gold and rainbow stone:

felt the sense of loss in that silly girl,
dead as a trilobite;
felt the pain that had gone into penetrating
the soft hyperbolic paraboloid of cartilage
that then displayed the decoration;
felt its sexual purpose:
to attract a dissimilar pattern of genes
to combine and recombine a trillion trillion times,
and become herself.

She briefly cherished the stone,
and returned it to its waiting.

## W. GREGORY STEWART

### *the button and what you know*

I this is the button and
what you know about it:

1. that it is a button—you know this.

2. that it has suddenly appeared before you.

3. that the button is
attached to a plate;
that the plate is attached to nothing else—
that it floats.

4. that this floating is taking place 2 feet or
half a meter in front of your immediate face.

5. wait—there is more.
the button and the plate are gray,
but not the same gray, each.
these are strange grays,
matte and yet translucent,
and fading, dark to light and back again.
first the button is dark, and then
the plate is darker, and although
the color changes are gradual and shifting,
the button and the plate are somehow never
the same gray at the same time.

it may be that this is important.

but it probably isn't.

6. beneath the plate, and likewise floating,
and having appeared just as suddenly,
and appearing just as oddly two-toned,
is a plaque bearing the words
ALL OR NOTHING.

7. oh, yes, a cylinder—there is a cylinder
floating vertically beside
the button and its plate

and the plaque beneath. it is light gray
at its bottom-most, and darker above;
you will notice over the next hour
that the light gray grows in extent—tomorrow
at this time you will notice
that the light gray takes up 1/7
of the total length of the cylinder,
and this will tell you something.
or should at any rate.

8. here is something else
that may—or may not—be important:
the button has appeared to you
on a crowded city street, and although
you are not alone, no one else
seems to notice the sudden appearance
of disenfixtured plates and buttons
and plaques and cylinders. or else
they do, but do not find it strange—
you yourself choose not to ask
anyone if they see these things,
even thought you *do* find them strange.

9. and this too—the gray configuration
remains before you no matter what direction
you go. this makes it all seem personal, somehow.
you do not dwell on this right now, but
within two hours your will find it fairly annoying.

10. one more thing—the cylinder floats to the left
of the plaque and plate.

it may be that this important.

but it probably isn't.

II. this is a part of what you do *not* know,
that might help:

1. a similar assemblage has appeared
to each of 26 individuals.
no two of these
live on the same world,
and of course no two worlds

are within the same galaxy.

2. note the use of the word 'similar'
in section II.1 above—in some cases,
what has appeared
is indeed a button, while
in certain others,
it is a toggle switch,
or a rocker switch,
or a touch pad. in two instances
it appears as things that I cannot describe.
I take on faith
that the function remains the same,
but I cannot guarantee this—
it *looks* like it, though.

3. although different languages—and
representations—are involved
the message stays the same: ALL OR NOTHING.

sometimes the concept is a single word.

sometimes it is not written
as you understand writing,
but is nonetheless transliterated
or recorded—audially, telepathically,
or psychotactilely. in any case—
ALL OR NOTHING.

4. none of you 27 is a leader of any kind.

5. no one of you is a scientist or theologian.

6. you are all unexceptional, and you have all
just recently lost your jobs. (coincidentally?)

7. here are the races of the rest of you.

first, those you might understand.

a. saurian.
b. cetacean.
c. canine, but unfortunately
too similar to the Chihuahua
to ever be made welcome at a Ho-Jo's.
d. bat. pink. and it swims.

e. rodent. hamsteroid, actually—its kind might
   eat a disobedient child simply to make a point
   to its surviving siblings
f. molluscan (octopuscan).
g. lemur.
h. elephant.
i. cetacean—this one is smaller, similar
   to a narwhale, but the tusk
   spirals in the *other* direction.
j. arachnid.
k. arachnid.
l. arachnoid. (note: there are too many
   spiders in the universe. I say this
   entirely without prejudice.)
m. Daffy Duck (you never even suspected, did you?)

next are those one step removed
from your own biologic.

n. an intelligent hollyhock whose greatest fear
   is premature pollination by a rogue bee.
o. a rogue bee.
p. manticore.
q. a streetcar actually named Desire.
r. a collective intelligence,
   the individual components of which
   look remarkably like spiders.
   (sigh . . . )
s. a bad attitude looking for
   a place to land—but it may be that you
   are more familiar with this than I suppose.
t. star maggot.
u. tuna surprise.
v. robo-droid, programmed to sell
   life insurance.

with the last you will have no common ground
or basis at all for understanding:

w. a silicate lump with career goals.
x. a rock, aging.
y. a pool of industrial waste that has outlived
   its creators.
z. something else.

8. each cylinder is calibrated
   to the local time appropriate to
   the place/space/displacement
   in which it has materialized,
   yet all are so synchronized
   that, when one finally becomes
   uniformly gray, all 27 will have become
   uniformly gray . . .

9. . . . which might suggest that time is running out.

10. the last thing that has anything to do with this
    that you do not know
    is what to do.

III. apparently you must make a decision:

   1. whether to push the button
   2. or not. to push. the button.

IV. you decide that you really need
   to think about what you know, and you are right.
   here are what you think about.

   1. ALL OR NOTHING. is that NOTHING
      if you push the button—
      or NOTHING if you don't?

   2. does NOTHING mean that nothing will happen—
      whatever you do—
      or that the universe as you know it
      will cease to exist? or something in between?
      or . . . (just give it a rest, will you?
      it's in there somewhere.)

   3. ALL presents similar problems; but at least
      you think you have a pretty good handle on OR.

   4. is all of this really happening, and if so,
      does it really *mean* anything—
      anything at all—
      let alone justify the cosmic paranoia
      that you are now just beginning to entertain?

   5. oh yeah—and why *you*, assuming sanity?

6. but even assuming anything else
   (and on the other hand), why not?

7. and, hey—who the hell is responsible for this,
   anyway? and are they sure
   they really want you? (and isn't *that* just
   'why you' again?)

8. well. maybe a decision isn't really required—
   perhaps you can just sidestep the issue.
   (and don't you believe it, Roscoe.)

9. what's the point?

10. what's for dinner?

V. after nearly a week of this, you finally decide
that you will push the button, and you suppose
that you must push it at the end of the week,
at precisely the same instant that the cylinder
goes uniformly gray. (yes—absolutely correct!
a good call on your part, by the way.)

you have decided to do this thing
because either you have gone entirely Bozoid and
it will therefore make no difference whatsoever
to universal cause and effect,
or you are entirely sane, and it might.

further, you have decided that only a benevolent entity
would have set up the game this way—
evil as you know it would have forced the issue
at first appearance, rather than giving you
a week to decide. well, you think—benevolent
or *incredibly* indifferent; nearly the same thing.
as it happens, you are spang-on
about the benevolent bit (but entirely wrong
to generalize about evil
as you have, given your limited experience; still,
no matter—the lucky guess is still correct.)

but you are not home free, not yet and not
by a long shot—because here's another thing
you don't know:

each of the 27 of you will have to push its button
at the same time as the others.
or else NOTHING, you see—
ALL OR NOTHING. (yes, I grant that a comma
after ALL would not have been amiss . . . but, then,
I didn't make the rules. did I?)

ok, ok—I'll tell you what the NOTHING part is.
the big NOTHING. the end. over, out, squat, kaput,
that's a wrap. time, space and all pints between,
done. that's all. auf flipping wiedersehn.

at any rate,
it is a good thing, that you decided as you have.

(now, at this point,
you may be wondering about the nature
of benevolence, given what I said before about evil.
let us address this:
benevolence within this context is giving you
the choice of allowing the universe to continue,
or of packing it in.
you see, at this end of things,
quite a number of potential neo-universes
and eager little possible creations
are shoving and crowding and elbowing their way
to the front of the line, blinking
in and out of existence and waiting for the next
Big Bang—but nobody else gets a turn until
whoever is IT is done. you see?
you don't? no, of course you don't - well,
it doesn't matter, anyway.)

VI. each of you has come to this same decision
(although of course you do not know this, because
you are unaware of each other's existence)—

each of you, that is, except
for one of the damned spiders (see—I *told* you!),
who is still waffling through it all . . .

VII. . . . while time is running out.

VIII. all right, all right, all right—

to make an interminable story less so,
the spider—at the last possible instant—
decides to hit its touch pad (and so
throw in with the rest of you, although
it doesn't know this), and the known
and unknown universes are saved.
at least for now.

IX. you know none of this, however. having pushed
your button, you only know that nothing
on your little planet and nothing
in your sorry little life
has changed. and you are right (and that
was the point of the exercise.) here are some things
that have not happened:

1. planets falling into their suns—
any more often than usual.

2. Planck time.

3. the sudden appearance of a transgalactic
black hole looking for a party.

4. the immediate and universal total decrease
of entropy.

5. or the opposite.

6. new age accordion recitals.

7. or anything much else out of the ordinary
for a vast and unencompassed creation.

X. but as I say—you know nothing of this. go home.
go to sleep. the button is gone.
you might find work tomorrow.

or you might not.

DAVID LUNDE

## *Song of the Martian Cricket*

I shouldn't come out here
so many nights, turning
my faceplate to the black sky
with the tasteless, artificial air
whispering in and out of my lungs—
the only sound besides the directional beep
from Marsbase below, a subaudial promise
of security, but not comfort.
It's not the pressure suit I mind
so much, not even the bottomless
black bucket of stars—I miss the moon
pregnant with promise, and the light,
grassy breeze coasting over the hill
to blow the soft strands of your hair
across my lips, and the sound of crickets
grinding their wings with need. Still,
I come out too often and stare
into the abyss of years, then rise,
feeling almost bodiless in the low gravity,
and drift back to the floodlit dome
small and forlorn beneath
its protective covering of dust.

WILLIAM J. DACIUK

# *To Be from Earth*

(From *The Journeys of the Night-children*, leaves XXIV-XXX, translated into the modern tongue by the scholars)

. . . and after many, many cycles of trying to reach out to the running, frightened creatures who lived so wastefully and unaware amid the blessings of that incredible blue treasure of a world, our missioners gathered themselves back into the great ship, and for one last time soared silently in long, looping arcs above the land, a final angry world-grazing flight born of bitterness, even of a not-unworthy jealousy.

And in one last gesture, they settled the great silver craft, idling quietly, in the wildest of that world's high places, in winds of cold, dry air, thin and sharp as fangs. There, in the rocks and the ice, they found the last of the great snow leopards, who looked back at them with the level eyes of a Watcher. On a whim, they granted her the gifts they had reserved for the others, not only that of True Speech, but also of Synthesis, and even Understanding.

And then they gathered around her, and sat right there on the snow, drawing their thin knees up to their chests, sheltering in the leeward curve of the still-warm acceleration hull.

And knowing what was wanted of her, the snow cat sat down as calmly as she could in their midst, and she wrapped her grand dappled tail once about, so ladylike, so Earthlike, she took the hunter's bite from her amber gaze, remembering that she too had once been a mother, and finding her new speech, she told them what she once told her long-ago cubs . . . .

To be from Earth means

that you live in a one-day world
where the darkness divides the light, and somehow
you must find that a blessing.

To be from Earth means
that you will walk
wherever you want to go,
even if the ice is sharp and it clings
to your pads, and it burns too cold on your tongue

to even think of licking it off,
and you know that your whole life long
no matter how fast you can go,
you will measure the times of all your days and paces
in the speed of that cold slow walk.

To be from Earth means
that even if you do not believe,
even if you rage and howl and bare your claws,
still you will one day, every day, go down
as far as you can
that long tunnel of prayer
until its adamant walls will narrow and press in against you,
and you know you are trapped and caught,
and yet you go back there for every tomorrow.

Above all,
to be from Earth means to know
that one day you must leave.
So you find your comfort in the wind,
you lose your anger in the hunt, you take your pain
right there in your arms
and you fold it
as many times as you can until
it becomes as light and meaningless as the north wind,
until you can balance it
like a feather on your paws,
and your friend, your wind, blows it away
and makes all your good-byes for you.

And in this there is madness,
but also much wisdom, the best of which says
that the moment is worth it.

And tired by the burden she had had to bear, the weight of sudden understanding, the sights and smells of that company so alien to her, the long and hard life in the mountains so soon to come to an end, her strength began to fail her, the great eyes closed, her head drooped and fell on her paws.

They wrapped a vapor of blue power around her, enough to sustain and comfort until she would wake. With a gesture they lifted their gifts from her; they carried her to the shelter of an outcrop of the hard blue rock that had defined her life in these hills. There they laid her down, and smoothed out her fur with their cold bare hands.

They returned here to the homeworld, on a pillar of fire forged from the quantum weaving among the thin keening spaces that separate the days of the weeks and the seasons of the years.

A good crew they were, but none ever voyaged again, strange to say. To a one, they retired to the brown wastelands below the Dry Ranges. Some say they practiced strange arts there, but the Father tells us No, they simply wanted to think by themselves, a skill our people had not yet developed.

In time, the great hives that had nurtured our race through its long and hard birth broke up, we abandoned the missioning voyages of our earlier cycles, we turned inward for many generations . . .

## Jane Yolen

# *Will*

The past will not lie buried.
Little bones and teeth
harrowed from grave's soil,
tell different tales.
My father's bank box told me,
in a paper signed by his own hand,
the name quite clearly: *William*.
All the years he denied it,
that name, that place of birth,
that compound near Kiev,
and I so eager for the variants
with which he lived his life.
In the middle of my listening,
death,
that old interrupter,
with the unkindness of all coroners,
revealed his third name to me.
Not William, not Will, but Wolf.
Wolf.
And so at last I know the story,
my old wolf, white against the Russian Snows,
the cracking of his bones,
the stretching sinews,
the coarse hair growing boldly
on the belly, below the eye.
*Why grandfather,* my children cry,
*what great teeth you have,*
before he devours them
as he devoured me,
all of me, bones and blood,
all of my life.

W. GREGORY STEWART & ROBERT FRAZIER

# *Basement Flats*

**Redefining the Burgess Shale**

You were downtime—one way on a simplex link
hoarding observations & lucky guesses
waiting to timeburn
back through the millennia, to where I waited
& read it all
(I called heads, you got tails—
they sent *you* down . . . )

*The creatures here are low form*
*bottom rung*

*true, but they too follow strict rules*
*mating habits that seem to mimic marriage—*
*or at least corporate law*

*love in this prehistoric age*
*is no less detailed*
*it is still a language of bump and run*

Downtime
doing Burgess reconnaissance
you got to see where the weird things are
you watched them die
you saw them settle
taking extensive notes for me to find later
I got to chip their carcasses from stone
time faxes I began to call them
a fossil is a time fax

*I find the water here*
*difficult to drink*
*no choice really but*
*my civilized stomach flora*
*are not adapted and I get sick*
*kind of the reverse of*
*savages lacking immunity to small pox*
*I hope in turn my germs are weak*

*the irony hurts*
*literally*

I remember the night before you left—
in our basement flat you said
*Anomalocaris* would be your favorite nightmare
I opted for *Opabinia*
we'd met as students, below ground then as well
re-cataloging the Walcott collection
in the Smithsonian dungeons
in the long flat trays & drawers & cabinets
oh, we innocently promised to redefine Walcott
& I remember how we hardly slept
that last night together—you drove alone
to the lab & the next morning you woke about
530 million years before I did
with no coffee

*Time paradox is not a simple matter*
*is it the paradox that history is immutable*
*I'm not sure*
*I feel I could change things easily—*
*though how is not yet clear to me*

You did the time well because
you did *time* well—
hell, better than I could have

*The true paradox may be that*
*whatever changes*
*timeburning might cause*
*are anticipated*
*and so the changes are there already—*
*or else how could I travel back*

& I studied what you lived each day
& I found your landmarks
& I found your fossils
& I found the phyla you found
we did good science together—
or so it seemed—
for a good long month

*I am pregnant*
*nothing is less a paradox*
*for it was by my will and choice*
*that it happened before my downtime*
*in case it was you going down*
*possibility swims before me*
*makes me dizzy with wavy lines*

Then came Retrieval
only they couldn't pinpoint you
& they didn't dare send me back
the project closed, bloody fools
"timeburning halted for investigation"
I wake up each morning
530 million years after you
to yet another day . . .

*My dear husband*
*soul mate*
*there are conventions which time*
*cannot account for*

*so*
*I'll not be seeing you again*
*(after two full months*
*that much is obvious)*
*I feel like emptiness distilled*
*who before has ever been this lonely*

*I have lost everything*
*I have no context for living*
*except my child*

Only last Easter, my wife
(& twenty Easters since I lost you)
did I think to do EMR/CAT
on the Walcott specimens
was there something we missed
inside, yes, inside the fossil remains
indeed
in just a few I found
these chips encoded with your notes
& with your personal entries
& your endearments

& too your thin gold ring
battered, worn to nothing
hardened in one
an *Anomalocaris*

*My concentrates are exhausted*
*I cannot sustain on these creatures*
*they do not agree*
*nor boost my energy*
*I fear I will not reach*
*the time to birth our baby*
*I've come this far and can't get that far*
*and I could have told her*
*or him, looking like you*
*I suppose*
*I could have said what no one can say*
*"your father lives millions of years*
*in the future"*

*paradox is a game, I have decided*
*a goddamned philosopher's convention*
*timeburning is possible*
*because all things are probable*
*blinking or not blinking—both*
*change history*
*whatever*
*goes unseen in the moment*
*or seen*
*is forever invaluable*

*each of us burns time*
*in a moment to moment speed chase*
*no matter the era*

*a big jump offers*
*no guarantee that it won't be another*
*basement flat back there*
*and poorly furnished*

*a bigger jump guarantees*
*no fucking special circumstance at all*
*except mortality*

I live in a penthouse now          one wall
is tiled in shale
I wear both bands—
you survived so long just to find me
once again
I am the change that you left behind

## Bruce Boston

### *Spacer's Compass*

South I shipped . . . galactic south
spanning the reaches of unbounded space
through the moss stars and beyond
hanging with this crew or that
a rough lot they were
or some just strange
stranger than you'd care to know
for a light year or two on the fly

West I wandered . . . galactic west
leaving lovers changing friends
past clusters hanging in the heavens
like burning ingots and bands of flame
landing always in a different land
a ready cup for alien ways
seeking never so much an answer
as a fix . . . a frame of reference
to sift my strangeness from

East I flew . . . galactic east
against the words of wiser souls
to decaying grandeurs steeped in fog
and cultures deadly spent
to language worlds and pleasure worlds
and the mother world or fabled so
a desolation of rust and snow
heir only to its past

Old I grow . . . galactic old
the polar night now calls my name
and still I tramp the stellar routes
from burning white to burning red
jump cutting lives and lands
fixing no frame of reference
beyond the passage itself
adrift in the passages
yet to be taken

Space has no directions
    and holds all directions at once
            a well of radiant possibilities
    all matter of strangeness

            . . . and the stars are for the living

## Jeff VanderMeer

### *Flight is for Those Who Have Not Yet Crossed Over*

You never thought
it could happen this way,
in a Guatemalan prison
among men armed
with rubber hoses, scalpels,
piano wire, and propaganda;
men who scream at you
to tell what you cannot tell,
until you mark the days by
the visits of your interrogators,
muttered prayers to God,
and the screams that echo
down the hall.

In a dream on a moonless night
it came to you from beyond the window,
mixed with the smell of palm trees,
sea salt, and rotting wood:
it came to you like a whisper
from your dead lover,
an exhalation of her breath.
You woke sprawled against
the wall opposite your bed
and the guard said, "Dios mio!"
It was a miracle, visitation,
the work of saints or devils.
You had flown around the cell
like an eagle, your arms
outstretched, fingers reaching
for the sky.

Miraculous, and yet you
laughed along with the guard
because to fly in your cell
cannot save you, because

the only flight you desire
is the flight of an angel,
spiraling upward, freed
from the sharp, clarifying
edge of pain.

DAVID LUNDE

## *Pilot, Pilot*

Your eyes were mirrors then,
silver as pressure domes, your
head raked back fifteen degrees.
The angle of your long neck
against the unwholesome horizontal
of that Port City street, the taut
cords of muscle straining
in my sweat-slick fingers,
are a senso I can't erase—
neither that image nor the shame,
knowing even then it wasn't you
I hated, brother, but myself, my life—
and at my back, suddenly the laughter,
hurrying near, the great laughter,
and you beginning to, your lips
beginning to crimp at the edges
just a bit as if to smile—you!
smile!—and I stared hard
at your eyes—at, not into—
trying to scan His approach
and afraid, so afraid to turn,
as if by not seeing straight-on
I would not be seen. But I was.

That fearsome hand, irresistible
and deft as a waldo, slipped loose
my grip, set us apart by a meter,
you cursing weakly, rubbing your throat
where my thumbs had bruised it,
both of us weeping like children
caught in some infantile squabble,
pulled casually apart and forgotten,
murmuring, "Easy, grounders, easy there."
Oh, easy, always easy for Him!
cruising off to His future,
off to His ships and His stars.

"But we made you!" I screamed,
and the fury was in me then, so huge
I flicked out blade and flung it
hard at His enormous back—
and how He did what He did then
I can't tell you; I couldn't see
but whirling flash and blur and hear
the shree-kaslam of its return.
Then He was gone. My blade
was buried to its hilt in a wall
of solid ferrocrete. The empty street
still echoed with His laughter.

I am not Arthur Pendragon
and have no hope. I suppose
I could have left Port City,
walked off those bitter streets,
but where is there to go
that matters? I can't forget
the mirrors of your eyes,
how they could not frame
His fearful symmetry, how they
diminished and diminish me.

## Dan Raphael

### *Skin of Glass*

surface that can be removed creates the problem of defining what's
underneath, having to go there

to find out, having to get the body involved, risk the senses, waste time
at least in cleaning up afterwards, in refuting the claims of others,
submitting
to spectroscopic analysis, finding experts in animal/vegetable/mineral
icons/remains/signatures

no skin but a seed, not a seed but an entrance, an entrance I can't fit,
a new body I must—a probe, an extension,
projecting several feet from
my skin my spirit coheres as a lazy gelatinous rectangle,
not what is made of but that it is, bigger but not more,
encasing more space not fed by molecular transmissions,
lacking the antennae to receive,
through the membranes where something meets nothing,
where meat sums not, things not, if so energized,
or shelled by that one way accretion

of filtering all I'm capable of, like a song in one key in half an
octave in four-four time,
a song that goes for fifteen minutes and can be repeated verbatim, a song
you can hear
twenty years away, on your ship to who know, one technology racing
another, hollow god-body-tree filled with too many fish
with refugees with poorly tanned furs,
an encyclopedia of non-seeding plants, spores in pores,
moisture interrupting everything,
thinning defining wanting
to make my brain a chalice

the hull is our roof protecting me from the rain below,
the rain that mostly can't escape
is sad amnesiac content,
salt is its gravity, fish are its wardens, its fantasies,
flying fish and diving birds, walking catfish and aquatic mammals,
huge subterranean pockets of symbiotic fungus displaying the colonic
intelligence of ants and bees,

rocks that appreciate their own beauty, molten substance
that can neither be defined nor predicted, where heat and pressure
create the same relativistic curves as speed and gravity,

the big bang is in each of us.
the periodic table is in each part of us.
the pantheon of buddhas, sattvas and bodhisattvas
are waiting around curves of the brain,
which is not in our heads but in our hearts
unfurling to the sun which is not in the sky
but everywhere
at once

## MARGARET B. SIMON

# *Variants of the Obsolete*

The observer is a gull. Or rather, it once
resembled the Aves, characteristically
retaining beaked nose and skeletal structure
with disproportionate forequarters.

It has positioned itself near a black hole
in the universe, or in time, whichever
you prefer. Sexless, oviporan, yet evolved
as a species capable of interchanging

mating roles. Nothing is impossible,
once certain genes have been successfully
manipulated (your father pooled his talents
in the Collective of '98) so you know

you are observing the observer,
the telescope you hold trembles
slightly, belying your great interest
in the scene you've trained to capture—

that unfolds too fast for you
to record (though all it takes is a
motion of your right digit)—you
forget—cursing fallibility

a flash of beak, a scalding light
so pure so white—you cannot focus.
In this instant, the gull bends
to the hole, extracting

what you believe is from another
universe. It tears the form to shreds
before your eyes; pauses before the last
morsel is swallowed, turns to face your 'scope.

You can hear it smile.

But you are not smiling. Your mandibles
clench, lock. Sweat beads on your forehead,
drying quickly in the arid breeze. You

reposition 'scope, this time with
shuttle ready for the holograph
record—but even as you

fuss and putter, willing as the human
beast is ever ready to perform—
the candid scene belongs to time; you
spit into the sand, disgruntled. Try

again, beating off the smaller birds
that flock around your equipment,
—-sparrows, jays, a flicker—
no admission. Turn on the buzzer, they
freeze, sizzle, fry, fall

build silent compost mounds around your
equipment. You kick the ashes with
plasti-booted heel, their acrid fluid
stains the pristine surface polish. In
disgust, you wipe the flakes

with gloved hand, disparaging of
tracing more today, yet from the distant
hill a strident laughter lures you—
surely one more shot at it, you think, you

hope, settling your 'scope again, into the
sun-white sand, surely this time it will
hold its prey, you'll see the form before
consumption resumes.

There is the land and the sea.
Then there are creatures from the land
and creatures of the sea. Before that
there was vegetation. Before the cycle
began, there were gases.

Digestive juices.
Items within the hole.

Your mouth waters. Endorphins can wait,
adrenalin flows, your fingers tighten
on the fulcrum module; it's set, you
find it there again, hunched expectant

vulturesque above the dark green-blue ball.
Silence. (you are aware of something flying
around your ears—you cuff at it with
the heavy glove, crushing the tiny wings.
it falls, distracting you a moment, for

it resembles a hummingbird—you toe it
into the sands with your boot)

Turn back to scanner, there it is—
yes, this time you have it on the
right way is to push this into play and
you'll have that little sucker

in focus what if you get scared what if
it looks like that is human, that thing
being caught like a fish or a worm or a
burp in time?

Yet there you go again. It's only a
piece of what looks like paper. You don't know
what's on the paper. The observer is taking off
with it. The observer blurs in your 'scope

Later, when you go over the recording, you
are able to enlarge the last shot. Your
equipment shows that the observer has a

blank piece of paper in its mouth.
You enlarge that paper ten thousand times.
In the exact center of the paper
you detect a black hole.

Possibly, you think, this was made by an ancient
typewriter, for the hole is precisely "O" shaped.

More logically, you surmise, this was a
computer error. So you return to your post
and wait for the return of the observer.

You wipe a few grains of dead sea sands
from your visor, return to view the horizon.
Shattering the still vista, acustualating
organs distinct, distant—the observer

sighted, sandprobes meet tympanic
membrane; you react, this chance
to purloin, document the Origin—
too dear—yet bothersome are

these small birds, who appear to
gather each time you prepare for
record; are they ectogenus, familiar
to their host, now hunched beside the
distant hole? No, you dismiss that—
concentrate on the

scene, the hole, the space where only
one observer finds and sits, where only
we/you/i/ the human part of this
totality of organismic world

is attuned to visit, to watch, to
gather and do as it will
with that which comes through
that goddamned hole nobody
knows, not even the best
of us they are all dead

your mind is wandering
they swarm about your faceplate
like wingless hummingbirds
faster, harder until

you use the buzzer. Scrape them off,
as bugs on windshield, yet without
a wind (you laugh, for there are
winds no more here) and why
and why again for the observer

is intent—the hole opens:
Slip-sliding from the portal to
infinity, it catches—

your gloved hand, still determinedly
attached to your mechanism.

You scream drowning in a vortex of wounds
wings, wind, whirling down to
meet the brightness not a tunnel

channel no a causeway flocked with
tiny denizens who

grasp you, suspend you above
the hole which is the "O" which is
the last whisperwish of Pharaohs
final gash of a shooting star
a young girl's blush when her
fingers found your erection

someone tunes a fiddle as
guitars duel, drums duet;
the stars are real
you are flying into the "O"

Which is the O which is the
mouthpiece of your visor. Beside you
sits the observer, the gull-creature

who will laconically
grasp you with dual phalanges
disperse your sight within ebon orbs
desensitize your awareness

confine you to infinite desolation.
And will it partake of you—bare essence
of what was once mortal?

You can hear it smile.

## BRUCE BOSTON

# *Future Present*

### A Lesson in Expectation

The future the past once envisioned is
nothing like the present we now inhabit.
No aerocars. No globed and spired metropoli.
No eccentric rube-goldbergian gadgets that
deliver a cool drink and a *shiatsu* massage
with the casual flick of a single switch.
No passage to the stars or even Mars.

And what of those gently purring walkways
lightly peopled by superior beings who glow
with the logic of a sublime moral grace?

Instead the present through which we slog
and stagger seems raw and tatterdemalion
as the past we expected to trash behind
—the twentieth is the cruelest century—
breeding sex plagues out of ignorance,
rife with demagogues and despoilation.

And while we ponder what roads not taken
have abandoned us to this frantic moment,
this vain dyspepsia of the modern mind
—no one answer, a gross on every side—
the tomorrow we envision is omnivorous:
mushrooming clouds, displacing populations,
devouring civilization with toxic fungal rains.

As those purring walkways recede and fade
into the dimming distance of the mind's eye,
the future, second by ever-rivering second,
oblivious to all expectation, yanks us bodily
into the coagulating rapids of its own design.

## TERRY A. GAREY

### *Spotting UFOs While Canning Tomatoes*

*for Karen Schaffer, Laurie Winter, and Eleanor Arnason*

First, get your tomatoes
this is not always as easy as it seems
if you are going to go to all that trouble
they might as well be good ones:
    red, full of flavor, perfectly ripe
    not a lot of bruises
grow them yourself
or get them from a farmers' market:
    Big Boy, Big Girl, Roma, Royal Chico
    Super Beefsteak, Early Pick, Lady Luck, Rutgers,
I've canned them all
just be sure they're good

pick a cool evening to do this if you can
unfortunately
cool evenings and tomatoes rarely go together
think of your pioneer grandmothers
indian grandmothers
slave grandmothers
immigrant grandmothers
putting up whole gardens for families of ten
and the hired hands

think of winter and canned tomatoes from the store
    tasting of tin
purse your lips in disgust
roll up your sleeves
and get to work
(a friend taught me to do this
long ago
when I was young and poor but had plenty of tomatoes
she put my tomato destiny in my own hands
as well as my peach, pear, applesauce and jelly destiny)

make sure you have enough jars, lids, rings and time
read through the instructions

(you know what your memory is like)
then fire up the canner and go for it

it's still the same hot water bath
taking too much room on the stove
a battered saucepan for scalding lids
bigger saucepan for scalding tomatoes
to make them easier to peel
then it's peel and core, my girl, peel and core
chop those tomatoes down
slip off the skins, keep the water hot

paring knife nicks, seeds spurt out
acids sting my skin
adds to the general redness

mere mortals should clear the kitchen
order out pizza—if they want to eat
it's like a marathon:
          sweat, determination, endurance
          going for the long distance—
          you have to remember to drink water
          so you don't dehydrate

as I go along, lift hot jars, dump water
push in the tomatoes, wipe the rims
leave a space for expansion
try to guess how much is enough
when I tighten down the lids
as I go along
          I philosophize
on the meaning of life
female bonding
female machisma
think about the farm women doing four times as much as this
every day all summer
and gasp, shake my head
I'll never understand how they did it

while the first batch boils I get ready for the next
try to stockpile against time and weariness
shift from one sore foot to another
wad up newspapers, wipe up flooding juice
save skins for the compost

I glance out the kitchen window and spot moving lights in the sky
an airplane, I think,
then as the steam rises around my head I realize
there are no flight patterns out my kitchen window
my hand clench, I think: UFOs, Flying Saucers,
aliens, green monsters
tentacled sentient creatures who need women to:
          can tomatoes?
The heck with them. Let them can their own tomatoes.

the kitchen's a mess
I've burned myself twice
used a bandaid
          scalded the inside of my arm with steam
but there are the first seven jars
and one by one
          ping!
          goes the beat of my heart as they seal down

take that, alien invaders

I work on into the night—not talking much—
hit a plateau
where it seems I'll never see the last bushel done
but finally
it's over
last jar is sealed
I dump the five gallons of hot water down the drain
so the canner won't rust
wipe down the counters
clean off the stove top
          touch once more all the women
everywhere, even outerspace aliens
who put something aside for winter

W. GREGORY STEWART

## *Day Omega*

*for Frederik Pohl*

maybe your mitochondria
will be left them on that day
(but even this day these
are not yours, really,
hitching their ride from
past to future with now
just another onramp on the way, and you
just another stranger
who stopped to pick them up,
as far as you're going,
if that will help),

but they will not think of you
as ancestor, any more
than you think of some barely formed
bit of organic twitch as ancestor,
or some tree-thing as ancestor,
eye-wide in the dark,
not like you think
of Grampy Joe, who still
has an appendix, or had one, anyway,
and five fingers and five toes,
each hand or foot,
they will not, could not
think of you that way,
even charitably.

oh, they are beyond day million, they
are so far past that, past human
and day billion and beyond,
you would not know them
for the fruit of the fruit
in their myriad forms
on worlds that do not even exist
in your time.

maybe your mitochondria,
that you'd picked up at evolution's yard sale
and handed on—that essence
of ape and earlier that's been in the family
for years (and now the great-grandchildren
don't know what to do with it),
maybe that strange life will still be there
on day Omega, hiding inside
and thinking the tiniest thoughts,
and smug, as the stars go out,

which is only as far as you were going, anyway.

LAUREL WINTER

## *why goldfish shouldn't use power tools*

first, they would probably be
electrocuted, as it is dangerous
to mix water and electricity.

*but what about battery power,*
you ask, *for example a cordless drill*
*with modified trigger,*
*sensitive enough to respond*
*to a filmy pectoral fin,*
*so that even an angel fish*
*could activate the bit?*
*I mean*—you say—*what about Navy S.E.A.L.s?*
*don't they use power tools underwater?*
*couldn't those be modified?*

well, yes, technically it could be done,
but think about it: your goldfish
swimming around in their bowl
atop your Louis whatever pedestal table
and an antique doily handed down from
great-aunt beatrice—who could have given you
a million dollars but no it was the doily instead—
those gold fish with a dazed expression
and vacant eyes and no cerebral cortex to speak of?
do you really want to give them
that kind of power? those kinds of tools?
think about it.
think about water damage
and how foolish you'd feel
filling out the insurance claim,
admitting that the bowl broke
because you empowered your goldfish,
gave them power tools and power over their destiny.
and how would you know
if one of your goldfish had a death wish?
it could be murder/suicide
and you would be an accessory.

*but what about goldfish rights?* you say
*what about the artistic possibilities,*

*the fine engraving they might do*
*on the inside of the bowl,*
*which i could then sell for a million dollars*
*—take that aunt beatrice—and what if*
*they're yearning for expression?*
okay, fine, expression is good,
but steer them in other directions.
how about performance art?
turn a video camera on the bowl
and give them the opportunity
to reveal their souls that way.
you can always tape over
the boring parts;
goldfish don't seem to understand
dramatic structure.
or power tools—
or the projected angst you are misdirecting.
you want a power tool? get one
for yourself.
buy the goldfish a plastic castle
and a bag of colored marbles,
or maybe one of those bubbly skeleton things
that goes up and down.
you want to give them
more than they need.
your own curved reflection
stares back at you
from inside the bowl.

## JOHN GREY

### *Explaining Frankenstein to His Mother*

His blinkered passion
has robbed him of much of
what you remember.
The Baron makes mockery
of your good and dutiful training
in the winding corridors,
the hundred and one frigid rooms
of that joyless castle.
He completely ignores
the rules and regulations
you drummed into him from birth
to when he slipped your net,
fell prey to the radical ideas that enmeshed
that accursed Swiss college tighter than ivy.
No, he has not followed the plot you wrote for him.
He seldom changes out of that
ragged coat, those faded gray pantaloons.
He does not pick up after himself,
not even the blood.
He is disrespectful of his elders,
especially the ultimate elder, God.
And, worst of all, he writes you no letters,
saves his quill for crazed diary scribblings.
He has become more a bleak personification
of his own crazed concept
than the well respected man of science you envisioned.
And worse, though he has not married
and settled down like the rest of your brood,
he has given you a grandchild,
a hideous thing made from
the flotsam and jetsam of corpses.
Unloved, it roams the landscape,
clumsily plunging misunderstanding
into terror.
"Life! I have created life!" was the
last thing he said to me.
An old saying of yours, as I understand it.

## Bruce Boston

### *Confessions of a Body Thief*

To take a stranger's mind
and wear a stranger's face,
to step into another's flesh
and claim a life in toto,
was a talent I discovered
at a raw and tender age,
when the world itself was
changing in unexpected ways.

Youth was in rebellion.
Generations ripped apart.
A war on foreign shores
and injustice on our own
soon led to cries of protest
and bloodshed in the streets.
Consciousness expanded like
a roiling mushroom cloud.
Those who offered answers
said it had to do with love

Amidst the fervor and the rage
I could have any life I chose,
from a pompous politician
feeding on the masses' needs,
riding high in limousines,
to a rail-thin rock idol
prancing on a concert stage
with women in the wings.
Flush with youthful vigor,
a burgeoning libido,
and a head full of ideals,
I promptly chose the latter
without a shade of doubt.

Wielding my axe like a pen,
and often like a sword,
I defined a shaggy credo,
my generation's song.

With the lyrics of another
I felt the wild exultation
of ovation upon ovation
and the instant adulation
that music can engender.
I lived my life so rapidly,
losing track of night and day,
the drugs within my veins,
time bunched and crushed
together like the jackknifed
cars of a derailing train.

When my body overdosed
I abandoned its dying shell.
After one or two false starts
I settled on my second host.
I became a cybernetic genius,
worked for IBM and Rand.
I calculated decimal points
to infinity and back again.
I'd never mastered logic
and never cared for math,
but I had another's brain
and a Ph.D. from M.I.T.
to think in algorithms
and converse with binary.

Abstract numbers galled
so I pursued the real sort,
the kind with dollar signs
that can buy a luxury yacht
to sail on the Côte d'Azur.
I was a Wall Street whiz kid,
a black belt of the exchange,
trading stocks and debentures
until I made a hundred million.
Then the junk-bond scandal hit,
and for the novelty alone
I spent a year in prison.

Once I surfaced as a woman,
more seductive than sin itself.
I learned what men will do
for the lust that they call love.

I learned how they'll compete
like fierce animals in heat
to possess a surface beauty
and caress a shapely thigh,
with no interest or concern
for whatever lies beneath.

I became a different woman
and fought for women's rights.
I battled like a termagant
with overblown executives
for an equal scale of pay,
for acceptance and promotion
on the corporation ladder
and all that should be mine.
The end result of this was
I soon became another man.

I've been brown and black
and white and yellow,
and all the shades between.
I've toiled stooped and sweaty
through the sun-baked fields.
I've sat in the awning's shade,
with a cool drink by my arm,
sporting an evil overseer's grin.
I've penned a best-selling novel
and composed a symphony.
Like a chameleon understudy
I have played most any part
as I moved across the stage
of this metamorphic age,
yet all of it soon paled
without my own identity.

I've cruised and skimmed
along the skin of things
like a surfer on a wave,
a rock skipping across a lake,
or a raindrop on a window
that reflects the room beyond
but can never find a passage
through the surface of the pane.

I've looked into the mirror
but never past my eyes.
I've only known my ego,
its desires and its needs,
the ocean's tidal roar
that belies the silent deep.

My future now stands open
like an endless avenue,
for every time I start to age
I seize on youth once more.
Yet is it worth the trouble
to keep changing hats and coats,
not in rhythm with the seasons,
just to please my petty whims,
when my soul is lost forever
in the shuffling and the rippling
of a hundred different skins?

If there is a kind of answer
that has to do with love,
if consciousness can change
and the world can follow suit,
I am not the one to judge.
I have stolen other lives.
I've ravaged mind and limb.
I have left my spirit far behind
and forsaken my own name.

## LAUREL WINTER

### *egg horror poem*

small
white
afraid of heights
whispering
in the cold, dark carton
to the rest of the dozen.
They are ten now.
Any meal is dangerous,
but they fear breakfast most.
They jostle in their compartments
trying for tiny, dark-veined cracks—
not enough to hurt much,
just anything to make them unattractive
to the big hands that reach in
from time to random time.
They tell horror stories
that their mothers,
the chickens,
clucked to them—
meringues,
omelettes,
egg salad sandwiches,
that destroyer of dozens,
the home-made angel food cake.
The door opens.
Light filters into the carton,
"Let it be the milk,"
they pray.
But the carton opens,
a hand reaches in—
once,
twice.
Before they can even jiggle,
they are alone again,
in the cold,
in the dark,
new spaces hollow

where the two were.
Through the heavy door
they hear the sound of the mixer,
deadly blades whirring.
They huddle,
the eight,
in the cold,
in the dark,
and wait.

## Geoffrey A. Landis

### *Christmas (after we all get time machines)*

Time machines, when they finally get invented,
        will be a real disappointment.
Turns out, you can't go backward
      —no trips to see Lincoln or the first Christmas
Only forward.

Soon they will be novelty items in the Sharper Image catalog,
   then Spencer gifts
        then K-mart
On sale this week only
(batteries not included)

Hiding Christmas gifts will become a snap:
No worry of junior sniffing out the hiding places.
      Wrap it,
      put it where the tree will be and
      */zap/*
to December 24, 11:59 pm.

Cleaning up Christmas decorations will be easy.
No need for a storage closet for sleds and lights and holiday socks
      the paperweights with Frosty and Rudolph
aim your time-zapper and
  */zap/*
      */zap/*
    */zap/*
they're gone,
back next December

reuse your wrapping paper,
      */zap/*
Day after Christmas
       */zap/*
your tree is already decorated next year.
the hand-blown crystal crèche
      */zap/*
(Don't move the furniture!
That table had better be in the same place next year!)

Snow? Why shovel?
    */zap/*
the kids will love it in August,

Christmas gypsies
*zap* themselves
to Christmas season, when there's always work in retail.
Christmas over, Christmas layoffs,
    */zap/*
and they're gone

And Christmas is nothing without the family
Grandma and Grandpa, getting along in years,
won't be here too many more Christmases
but
    */zap/*
Besides, once a year
it's sure cheaper than a home.

And some of us,
    weary of cheerless cheer
        tired of malls
            sick of Christmas lyrics ringing in our ears
            will,
        at last,
    escape.

*/zap/*

## Rebecca Marjesdatter

### *Grimoire*

As a child I believed
that if I read a book cover to cover
without missing a word or skipping
a single line ahead,
a spell would take me inside the tale—
no enchanted rings or magic wardrobes required.

I kept the faith, through five thousand failures.
As an adult, however, I have learned the secret.
I will write the stories myself.
I will write myself into the stories.
Write, until there is nothing left of me at all.

And someday, a reader will remove
that binding from a dusty shelf
and find among the gatherings, desiccated,
like a pressed bouquet of anemones and violets,
pieces of myself:
wispy locks of wavy hair,
translucent scraps of skin,
a tiny, curled, fleshless hand, like a sparrow's claw,
lodged between pages stained with russet ink.

## Joe Haldeman

# *January Fires*

27 January 1967

precisely one month before I'd leave for Vietnam

the TV went silent

we all looked      into the white noise

news bulletin
the Apollo One astronauts
Grissom   Chaffee   White
have died in a freak fire

(killed by pure oxygen and one spark
on a wire's cheap cotton insulation)

no pictures   please   no pictures

years later   tempered by combat   I saw those grim
unheroic pictures      ugly and real as napalm death

one almost got the door open

28 January 1986

Daytona Beach
tropic morning   winter cold
rigid splash of icy breakers

freezing seabirds
stalked annoyed
on cold sand

three launch holds   no more patience
coffee cold and bitter   gritty
waiting and grit and cold
that's all we talked about
talking to keep warm

it finally went up

six jocks and one school teacher

riding a white column of steam

to a solid spasm of fire

cloud tombstone on the edge of space

the tourists cheering madly   madly
thinking it was a part of the show
booster separation or   the rest
whatever they call it   of us
in shock

watching the pieces fall
into the frigid water

no parachutes   no parachutes

two hours later   numb
the resident expert   I sat down in front of a microphone
and the pale talkshow woman
asked whether I would still go up

sure   I said   twenty-five to one odds
did you ever draw to an inside straight
and did you expect to make it

while something inside

still stalking jungle trail

said   liar   liar   lair

you know

you would kill anything

to stay alive   you

would even kill a dream

## Bruce Boston

## *My Wife Returns as She Would Have It*

*for Maureen*

"I'd come back as a butterfly,"
she often told me, "a Monarch
or something equally as beautiful."

Eleven days after her death it happens.
I am walking a block from our house
when a quick flutter of velvet wings,
dark against the pale dome of the sky,
passes left to right inches from my face,
causing me to pull up short in mid-stride.

Turning to the right I see a butterfly
has landed on the sidewalk at my feet.
Black and brown shadings striated by
vermilion bands, speckled with white.
(Not a Monarch but a Red Admiral,
I later discover in one of her books.)

"Is that you, sweetheart?" I whisper.
I am a fifty-six-year-old man suddenly
kneeling on the cement spilling out
his love and regrets to a lone insect
he hopes is a reincarnation of his wife.

Clearly as beautiful as any Monarch,
an epiphany of color in my flat world,
the butterfly appears to be listening.
Brilliantly hued wings shift slowly
up and down as if they sense the
coarse human sounds filling the air.

Even once language deserts me,
it/she remains a moment by my side
(together like partners after a dance!)
before soaring into a sky all-at-once blue,
vanishing into her future and my past,
alive and free as our finest memories.

## Lawrence Schimel

### *How to Make a Human*

Take the cat out of the sphynx
and what is left? Riddle me that.

Take the horse from the centaur
and you take away the sleek grace,
the strength of harnessed power.
What is left can still run across fields,
after a fashion, but is easily winded;
what is left will therefore erect buildings
to divide the open plains, so he no longer
must face the wide expanse where once
his equine legs raced the winds
and, sometimes, won.

Take the bull from the minotaur
but what is left will still assemble
a herd for the sake of ruling over it.
What is left will kill for sport,
in an arena thronged with spectators
shouting "Olé!" at each deadly thrust.

Take the fish from the merman:
What is left can still swim,
if only with lots of splashing; gone
is the smooth sliding through waves,
alert to the subtle changes in the current.
What is left will build ships
so he can cross the oceans without
getting his feet wet; what is left won't care
if his boats pollute the seas he can no
longer breathe, so long as their passage
can keep him from sinking.

Take the goat from the satyr
but what is left will dance out of reach
before you have a chance
to get that Dionysian streak of mischief,
the love of music and wine, the rutting parts

that like to party all the day through.
What is left will be stubborn and refuse
to give way; what is left will lock horns
and butt heads with anyone who challenges him.

Take the bird from the harpy
but the memory of flying, a constant yearning ache
for the skies so tantalizingly distant,
will still remain, as will the established pecking orders,
the bitter squabblings over food and territory,
and the magpie eye that lusts for shiny objects.
What is left will cut down the whole forest
to feather their sprawling urban nests.

At the end of these operations,
tell me: what is left? The answer: Man,
a creature divorced from nature,
who's forgotten where he came from.

WILLIAM JOHN WATKINS

## *We Die as Angels*

We die as angels and come back as men.
No consolation that we chose to die
or that we only die to die again
or that our dying proves all death a lie.

We go to rescue others trapped in Time
lost angels dazed and blinded by despair,
who can't remember life in the Sublime
and wander angels still but unaware

and think themselves mere things with lives so brief
one melancholy wail could tell it all
trapped in the maze they build by their belief
obsessed by Bliss they cannot quite recall.

We go to wake them, but we pay the cost
that we agreed to pay before we came,
that though our sacrifice will save the Lost
we cannot go back home again the same.

Mere angels who know only perfect Bliss
who have not died to men and back again
know nothing of the taint of Time's abyss
cut off from us by what we know of pain,

turn from us there where Love and Glory sings
and hide their faces from us with their wings.

CHARLES SAPLAK & MIKE ALLEN

# *Epochs in Exile*

**A Fantasy Trilogy**

*One: Reflections on a Far Shore*

I, Kaetzal, Claw of Drakhoun, walk this far shore, alone.
Baleful sun fires the horizon of the quiet sea; one moon,
Alone, silvers the jungle at my back. Starfarer no more.
Here will I go insane. The exile pod floats beside me,
Distortion waves shimmering off the gravity shifter. It can
Take me anywhere, but would shatter were I to challenge this
Sky. It cannot be reprogrammed. Disruptor, exoskeleton,
Metabolic batteries, resonator—I've enough tools to name
Myself King—of this forsaken dustspeck of a world.
A serpent glides through the slime at my feet, jeweled back
Sparkling in moonlight. I see myself, three thousand years
Hence: a belly crawler, naked and unthinking, a taster of
Mud. I finger my disruptor. Shall I Kill this serpent,
Punish it for mocking me? Shall I teach it who is King?
A shorebird circles the surf, hunting, silhouetted on the
Smooth blue moon. Should I Kill all? I could cleanse
This world, were I so inclined. But why should any be
Allowed to die before I do? The Elders locked within my
Code a new template—eggs, sperm, rebirthing rhythm—
I am now a self-replicator, like a fungus.
This they called Mercy . . .

What shade the Drakhoun sky tonight? What pattern the five
Moons? What tale throbs through The Dreamsong, now that
Kaetzal, lone voice of discord, has been silenced? Angry, I
Shed the exoskeleton, drop it into the mud. Why wear
Another prison? Before two steps I collapse to my hands and
Knees, crawl in circles, humiliated, my punishment complete.
A crude chorus trips my resonator—one could hardly call
These minds at all. I strain to peer into the jungle.
Tribes of mangy apes—no, not so pure as apes—another
Thing—human. I reach for the disruptor, to reduce them
All to sand—but no. Instead I show them a little trick
I've learned, a quirk of this oxygen-rich world.
I breathe fire.

Scurrying, they leave a ghost in my resonator—a serpent
God, shedding skin, breathing fire. Laughing, I place my
Exoskeleton and disruptor in the pod, send them over the sea
To shatter, fire announcing a new legend, lord, and exile.
Earth's Sole Dragon, I set forth. My tiny universe beckons.

*Two: Wetborn in Winter*

I ache for the Sun. I will not see the Spring.
Every century or so, I've learned, Winter smashes these
Mountains, and snow falls for weeks. This is such a storm.
The cave mouth has iced over. I'm so still and cold, the
Ice could be within my bones. I groan, and moist,
Warm breath creates a spiral aperture in the ice disc
Closing me in, a crystalline iris which shifts and swirls.
Through this I peer, hoping to glimpse a starry sky
Beyond this blizzard. Is it right to long for home,
After so many centuries? Is it good to ache for my bright,
Warm life, on The Homeworld, so many galaxies away?
There is too much time to think in winter.
And this winter is different: Another is here.

Time, heavy as miles of ice. Though I'm chilled, Another is
Warm, swaddled in my beating heart, shifting and wriggling
In my clean blood. When I was my mother, did I resent
Myself so? Excruciating destroyer, ignorant, selfish.
I writhe around my cave, bleating and bellowing. My cries
Shatter ice, hurl avalanches through chasms.
Do grannies in the village below soothe babies with whispers
Of Old Tseng Chen, whose cries echo around the moon?
There is no time to think. One has awakened.
I don't know that a claw is slicing through my chest
Until I look down and see it. Paralyzed, I watch
My body split, my blood pool on the cave floor.
A jeweled serpent, fifteen feet long, splashes free.

Its scales harden as it licks my blood from the floor.
Panting, I wish to scream, but hold my breath for fear
I'd burn the exquisite murderer. It finds my open chest,
Gnaws there, moves to my throat. I stare at the cave mouth,
Unfeeling, and fancy distant stars. Soon it eats
Through my eye. It gnaws through the socket, and for only a
Moment, the pain is fabulous. Then it is upon my brain.

Darkness, and sleep, until I awaken, eating this bloody gray
Bread. I look to the cave mouth and wonder: What are stars?

I return to this strange feast, this mountain of icy flesh.
I breathe fire, slink between blackened bones like a cage
Of the past. Days and nights pass—I know, I remember:
Someday the ice will break, and I will see the Spring.

*Three: Thoughts Before the Slayer*

Marvelous and tiny, yet another approaches. Wasn't it just
A decade ago when the last ventured here? Or was it a
Century? These things blur together. Regardless, another
Approaches, his heart throbbing, daunting my ancient ears,
Hand-hammered armor clanking and creaking, brittle iron
Sword held aloft, resonating in the wind.
    And me?
Too weary to tell him of my legends, memories really,
Learned not at a granny's knee, but gnawed from the inside
Of my dead mother's skull when I was wet-born, as she had
Gnawed them from her mother's, and so on, so many times on
This earth, beneath this sun.

He stops; kneels; a prayer to whisper, his pious words
Whipped away by the wind.

I slide along the rock ledge before my cave, wish for more
Sun—how I've always loved this sun. Should I interrupt
His prayer to talk about this sun, or talk of cool blue suns
I remember? Or great red suns which fill strange skies, cast
Shadows on castles which were old when his race was young?

He continues to pray, this creature come to kill me. My
Teeth hurt. I cannot bear the thought of eating. Some days
I can't breathe fire, and my own smoke chokes me. My heart
Hisses within my chest, and worst—there are no eggs.
I welcome him, this tiny knight, but also want to tell of my
Line, how one thousand, seven hundred, and sixty-three lives
Ago my First arrived, sent his starship to the ocean floor.
How I've watched since then, seen these tiny unscaled ones
Stand up from the ape, construct cathedrals. How when first
I saw a war I could have scoured this Earth clean, set fire
To the sky. How when first I heard a lullaby cooed in a
Cold cave, I knew this race would prevail . . . .

His prayers are done. What name his god? Or should I ask
His name—Saint George, Glooscap, Sigurd? Or ask which of
A thousand names he calls me—Nidhogg, Draconis, Hydra?

He arises, steps forward, sword drawn, fear and courage in
His eyes. I roll over in the warm sun, on this world grown
Too small for legends. He targets my breast, pale and
Penetrable, while I wonder what will be said, when his
Descendants meet my ancestors, out among the stars.

## Sonya Taaffe

# *Matlacihuatl's Gift*

Be wary when you kiss her: which mouth
you choose to press your lips against
when you meet her in the highlands
where she walks alone. By roadsides,
by moonlight, sway of hair falling dark
down her sinuous back, her steps hold
the grace of shadows, panthers,
and under your touch her skin breathes
like a flower. Be careful when you approach her
as she awaits you in the dark,
when you slide one hand beneath
her riverbed hair, whispering the words
that lovers and liars always use:
por favor, querida, nunca más and siempre,
calling on time and all eternity
to hold fast your love as you lay her down
silent where her arms wind around
your back, where her mouth fits to yours,
where you cannot resist her and she never
says no. Her beauty burns the mind.
Printed with your kisses—lip and cheekbone,
throat and palm, vulnerable nape of the neck
when you push her hair aside to taste
the second mouth she hides there,
flowerlike, no more a mouth than what
she keeps between her earth-warm thighs—
moving on you like the tide, she holds you
tight so that you cannot see, as you cry out
into the hollow of her tawny throat,
what smile her face wears in the aftershock.
No time for wariness or regret
when you have left her, under trees' shadows
at the roadside, when you have kissed
both her mouths and burst stars within her
and lied your love to her in the dark:
down in the cities again, you wonder
what made her laugh as you walked away,

why she folded your hand over the coins
you tried to press into her palm, freeing
your fingers with a gesture that almost
pulled you back. Did she foresee
this nausea in the morning, these twinges
in your belly as though a salt sea
shifted within you, while you check
your weight and frown, resolve to drink
less beer and work out more—and you want
to eat the oddest things—does she know how
you never dream her face except smiling,
close-mouthed and confident, sideways
step over what you thought you knew?
Her coin is reversal; she inverts
the mirror, pays you out
in the shadow side of common knowledge
until you no longer recognize where she began,
where you end, until you understand
what she gave you when you took from her,
in nine months' time, to overturn your world.

RUTH BERMAN

## *Potherb Gardening*

Now a garden for the craft,
Said the witch,
Needs fertilizing, same's you would
Your roses or your kitchengarden—
Same, I mean, except, of course,
You want special dung for special gardens.

Unicorn-soil gets rid of poisons
Spreading from your upas tree.
It also discourages rabbits and tent-worms.

Mermaid-soil's good for marshes.

Roc-soil will encourage your aconite
And cloudberry or yellowrocket or wingwort—
Anything you plan to stir in flying potions.
Griffin-soil's good, too,
Phoenix if you can get it,
But it's pricey,
And if it's offered in a catalogue,
It's probably not the real thing, anyhow,
I don't care how old and established and reliable.

Don't use dragon-soil—
It'll burn the roots
Even of fireweed and flame trees.

Fairies, now, say they don't produce
And no use asking—
They're too ethereal,
Too above that sort of thing.
Where they've been dancing, though,
You get good mushrooms.

THEODORA GOSS

## *Octavia is Lost in the Hall of Masks*

The Mask of Inquiry asks: Why are you here, Octavia? The linens have been spread for the wedding feast. The glasses have been filled with yellow wine. A roasted pig lies in its bed of parsley, squabs lift their legs in paper caps between turnips carved to resemble roses. The wedding guests are waiting to toast the bride.

The Mask of Elegance says: The Duke sits beside an empty chair. There is a collar of Flanders lace beneath his receding chin, there is a boot of Spanish leather on his club foot. A ring of gold and onyx has slipped from his finger. His chin has dropped and his lips are slightly parted, as though to ask a question. Surely he is asking where you are, Octavia.

The Mask of Confusion says: A fly wanders over the breast of a Countess, and she does not brush it away. The page boys lie with their legs tangled, like lovers.

The Mask of Propriety says: There is blood on the hem of your petticoat, which ought to be as white as snow, as bone, as virginity. There is blood on the hem of your dress, and blood on the seed pearls sown in an arabesque across your train. There is blood beneath the fingernails of your right hand.

The Mask of Flattery says: You are beautiful tonight, Octavia. Your hair, piled on your head in ringlets, shines like a nest of little black snakes. Your eyes are the color of rusted coins, your neck the color of old ivory.

The Mask of Skepticism says: Yes, you are beautiful, like something dead.

The Mask of Nostalgia says: Ivy grows over the walls of your father's castle, leaves rustling where sparrows have made their nests. Bubbles appear on the surface of the moat, and you wonder what lies beneath the lily flowers. You dip your toes into the green water. A trout rises to the surface, flashing its dark iridescence, and then sinks again. In the distance, cowbells chime, low and irregular.

The moon rises.

Your shifts are laid in chests scented with lavender. Your bed is spread with sheets of ironed linen edged with lace. They are marked with a red spot from the first time blood ran between your legs.

The moon is touching the tops of the chestnut trees. You enter the grotto where you first lay down for the gamekeeper's boy.

The Mask of Seduction says: The thief is waiting for you in the forest. His lips are thick and the backs of his hands are covered with black hair. His grip will bruise your wrist, his filth will rub off on your body.

The Mask of Longing says: He will tickle the insides of your thighs with a knife.

The Mask of Perception says: The thief with eyes like the backs of mirrors was once the gamekeeper's boy.

The Mask of Accusation says: You have poisoned the wine, Octavia. You have poured a white powder into the glasses. The wedding guests have drunk in careful sips. How silently they sit, how very still.

You have stabbed the Duke, and licked the knife you stabbed him with. You have spit blood and saliva on his cheek. It runs down and stains his collar with a spot of red.

The Mask of Consequences says: The knife is still in your hand, Octavia. Put it to your wrist, peel back the skin as you would peel a damson plum.

The Mask of Fragmentation says: Your wrists are streaming away in red ribbons. Your dress falls like confetti. Your corset disintegrates, and moths of white silk flutter through the corridors. Your waist cracks, your torso crashes on the floor. Your hair writhes like little black snakes, then crawls into hidden corners. Your nose breaks, like the nose of an Attic statue. A breeze blows away your left ear.

Only your mouth remains. It parts and attempts to speak without teeth or palate or tongue, saying nothing, not even stirring the air.

ROGER DUTCHER

## *Just Distance*

"Just distance," she said.
"Not mad, not dislike, not hate";
the moon is bright and the
Perseids meteors pale,
as I contemplate "distance."
The Earth, perfectly positioned,
would boil at closer than
93 million miles distant,
and freeze if farther away.
The moon moves our oceans
and its reflected light
suffuses our poetry and songs,
yet any closer and we would be
torn apart by its gravity.
Somewhere, Comet Swift-Tuttle
moves, cold and dirty.
Only briefly does the solar wind
cause it to flare into beauty,
then, as it moves away,
and the distance grows, it
enters again, its cold, long orbit
so far from the sun.
Yet the debris it leaves
produces this beauty and
each year I watch
as one by one
the meteors are consumed
in the distance they fall.
"Just distance," she said,
not realizing that distance is all,
and yet no distance is greater
than that between human hearts.

# Afterword

## *Suzette Haden Elgin*

When I founded the Science Fiction Poetry Association in 1978, I had very broad reasons and very narrow goals. I had noticed that people interested in science fiction poetry seemed isolated; at conventions, you saw them all alone in corners reading strange-looking publications or scribbling on tiny scraps of paper. I had a vague general idea that I should do something to at least make it possible for them to identify one another and stay in touch, such as starting an organization and providing it with a modest newsletter.

This didn't strike me as a large or difficult task. I was sure that I'd be doing well if I could rustle up 25 members and keep 20 of them longer than a year. I was at that time a busy assistant professor at a large California campus (not the kind where the prof only sees two graduate seminars, each containing four people); I had five children at home and a house to run; I was moonlighting in various ways; and I had a writing career to see to. It seemed to me that I could just barely manage the amount of correspondence and interaction that would be needed for a 25-member organization with a mimeographed newsletter stapled in one corner for mailing. And from that position of ignorance, I wrote a first issue, called it *Star*Line*, ran off fifty copies, sent them out to likely candidates, and waited.

I was wrong on all counts, of course. In the first place, the amount of work necessary for a 25-member SFPA, with a newsletter that published and reviewed poetry as well as fulfilling service functions, was far too much for any one person to do unless it was the only work they were doing. I had never suspected that. In the second place, there turned out to be far more than 25 willing and energetic members; 150 to 200 was the accurate number. Very soon, even with the publication of *Star*Line* held to every other month, I found myself in serious trouble and contemplating closing the whole thing back down again.

But fortunately, others (especially Maureen Kaplan and artist Karen Jollie) stepped forward to save SFPA and take all the hard work off my hands. In the next few years—the early 1980s—a lot of work got done. Author Elizabeth Chater volunteered to serve as our first president, and I wrote an informal constitution which the organization adopted, mainly by not protesting it.

Soon after its founding, SFPA established an annual award for the best short science fiction poem (up to 49 lines) and the best long one (50 lines or more) of each year. We wanted to call it something as unique as "Nebula" or "Oscar," not a generic name like "the SFPA Best Poem of the Year Award." With Robert Heinlein's kind permission, we were able to follow a member's suggestion and call it the Rhysling Award (pronounced "Riseling"), after the Blind Singer of the Spaceways in Heinlein's classic, "The Green Hills of Earth."

SFPA members may nominate one poem in each category, and the nominated poems are published in an annual *Rhysling Anthology* with a ballot enclosed. (This means that when SFPA members vote for a Rhysling Award they have had the opportunity to read all of the nominated works; the only exception has been in rare instances when we could not obtain permission to reprint a particular poem.) The first Rhysling Anthology (with a cover collage done by me) was photocopied and stapled in one corner; I still have the collage.

SFPA also began an active campaign to establish science fiction poetry as a valid genre and to open markets for it. Those of us who attended science fiction conventions and writing conferences (or any other appropriate function) put on poetry panels and readings and workshops as often as anyone would let us. We took samples of *Star*Line* with us to public meetings and displayed them, to get the word out; we held SFPA meetings and room parties and invited anyone interested to attend. We wrote letters to the editors of science fiction publications asking that they begin carrying poetry if they did not already do so, and doggedly submitted science fiction poetry even to editors who gave us only tepid and tentative maybes. A number of our members published science fiction poetry journals of their own, and poetry collections and chapbooks of their own; some of our members received grants to carry out projects in science fiction poetry. We produced a cassette tape of members reading their own poems and offered it for sale.

Many volunteers, several of them accomplished poets, labored to keep SFPA alive through the years. At a time when I found myself unable, even with so much help, to maintain the standards of service to which SFPA members were entitled, poet and editor Robert Frazier took over my duties, with almost no notice. Bob not only served two stints as editor of *Star*Line*, but kept the organization running when there often was no titular President. In the 1990s, during poet and artist Marge Simon's presidential term, the SFPA drafted its first formal constitution and gave its first Grand Master Award to prolific poet Bruce Boston, a seven-time Rhysling winner. Many others have lent a hand, and there have been bumps and joggles from time to time, but *Star*Line* is alive and well, and the SFPA is more active than ever before.

We now have a community of science fiction poets and a forum (three forums, now that there's also a website and a listserv) where they can communicate with one another. The letters columns in *Star*Line* and e-mail exchanges on the listserv have not been just lively, they have been passionate; and many issues have been wrangled there at the top of our collective lungs.

We are not going to see a science fiction poetry equivalent of *Paradise Lost* on the best seller lists in my lifetime—although I have lived to see the publication of book-length science fiction poetry, and that is definitely progress. But thanks to the hard work and cooperation of all our members, SFPA has brought science fiction poetry out of those isolated corners.

During this time, 46 poets have received Rhysling Awards for 61 winning poems. I think the award is respected in the sf community, especially because every member has the opportunity to read every nominated poem before voting; this is unusual and means that we can really say that the poems chosen represent the judgment of the entire voting membership.

The SFPA is now 28 years old, and has survived and grown and made much progress toward its goals. We would welcome your membership and your participation, as it continues to grow.

## About the Authors

**Duane Ackerson** (1978, 1979) is the first back-to-back winner of a Rhysling award. He edited an early anthology of speculative poetry called *Rocket Candy*. He says of "Fatalities": " . . . a clock under a glass dome on the mantelpiece . . . looking at it, I heard the phrase, 'striking the hour' [and] had the cartoonish image of the clock's arms striking hours, and those hours piling up on the mantelpiece." "I was intrigued by the idea of trying to recapture a more childlike hold on my imagination by looking at words and phrases in as literal a way as possible." Of "The Starman" he says: "The theme of the outsider or displaced person (perhaps because I was an "Army" brat and lived in a multitude of places) has always had special poignancy for me. I recall wanting to catch some of this feeling in the poem. It seems the poem started first thinking about the lot of that star traveler, then... the image of the dandelion in bloom and how the spores scatter . . . " He resides in Oregon.

**Mike Allen** (2003) is editor of the speculative poetry journal *Mythic Delirium*. He has published in a wide range of genre publications and has been actively involved with the Science Fiction Poetry Association, including being its President. He is co-editor of this volume. He says of the poem done with Charles Saplak: "I recall a two-hour session (or longer?) spent in . . . [Charlie's] den . . . going over the whole poem word-by-word, arguing over phrasing, placement of line breaks, order of lines, all for the sake of bringing Kaetzal's lonely journey to life." He lives in Virginia.

**Ruth Berman** (2003) says of her poem: "A few years ago I suggested a panel on witches for Arcane, a local (Twin Cities) convention usually held around Halloween—and then didn't take part in it, as I'd gotten the dates mixed up, and was out of town that weekend. The fear of witches that has been manifested by objections in recent years to even the idea of a good witch (along with attempts to ban Baum's *The Wizard of* Oz or Rowling's Harry Potter books) seems so downright weird, that a non-phobic portrait of a witch seemed an attractive idea, and as I didn't take part in the panel, I tried a poem instead." She lives in Minnesota.

**Michael Bishop** (1979) not only extends his unique vision to fiction, but to his poetry. In addition to the Rhysling, he has won the Clark Ashton Smith Award for verse as well as the Nebula & Locus Awards. He lives in Georgia.

**Bruce Boston**(1985, 1988, 1989, 1994, 1996, 1999, 2001) is the first (and thus far only) Grand Master of the SFPA. He has become one of the most well-known and popular poets in the genre. He has won the Rhysling Award more times than any other poet. He has also won the *Asimov's* Readers' Choice and Bram Stoker Awards for poetry, and the Pushcart Prize for fiction. His poems cover a wide range of styles, from science fiction to horror, and explore not just outer space, but inner space. Trying to encapsulate a summary of his winning poems in a small space is particularly difficult. From actual events, memories and hopes of childhood, the real and terrifying events in our world, dreams, and the inspiration of television programs, Bruce has woven a body of work as varied and rich as any poet. He says of his poetry: "Some poems operate like spontaneous combustion. They appear out of nowhere and write themselves." He also says: "To say something is 'only a dream' is to dismiss it as inconsequential. 'In the Darkened Hours' attempts to assert the importance of dream events in our lives . . . ." He lives in Florida.

**G. Sutton Breiding** (1990) says that his poem is: " . . . a meditation on beauty, romance, death, eros; and the nature of poetry itself, of which, what can possibly be told? Any attempt to explain the origins of poetry or the impulse to write it is foolish, futile, and above all, vain. The ecstatic act of writing itself is all that matters at day's end. And even that is illusion, however glorious its secrets." He lives in West Virginia.

**Siv Cedering** (1985) was born in Sweden. In addition to poetry she also writes children's books and novels. She paints, composes and is also a visual artist. Her most recent book is *Letters from an Observatory: New and Selected Poems, 1973–1998*. She lives in New York.

**Adam Cornford** (1983) teaches at a small university. He has published several collections of poetry including *Animations* from City Lights Books. He resides in California.

**William J. Daciuk** (1993) has been involved with the SFPA for many years, and was mostly responsible for creating the association's current governing constitution. He coordinated the annual *Rhysling Anthology* in 1991.

**Ray DiZazzo** (1982) says of his poem: "I've always gotten great satisfaction from exploring unusual perspectives. Consider the idea that entire worlds or layers of perception may be evolving around us at speeds so tremendously fast or slow they're invisible. Simplicity is a must for me . . . I feel my work has to deliver with understatement and simplicity in order to transcend the page." He lives in California.

**Sonya Dorman** (1978) was one of the first winners of the Rhysling for best poem. She was born in New York and spent time in Maine before moving to New Mexico where she died. Her poetry appeared in numerous journals, including Virginia Kidd's seminal *Kinesis*. She was a part of the Milford writing group and was friends with Thomas Disch, Ursula K. Le Guin and numerous others. She is included in the anthology *Burning With a Vision*. In addition to her poetry she also wrote prose and was nominated for a Nebula Award and appears in the famous Harlan Ellison anthology, *Dangerous Visions*. She is the first Rhysling winner to pass away. (1924 - 2005)

**Ken Duffin** (1981) loves blues music, The Marx Brothers, The Detroit Pistons and Arsenal FC soccer club. He lives in Canada where he is a youth worker, coach and chess tutor.

**Dutcher, Roger** (2004) is the editor of *The Magazine of Speculative Poetry*, which he co-founded with Mark Rich. He is also co-editor for poetry for *Strange Horizons*, an online SF zine. He says of his poem: "Often SF poems deal in artificial settings. This poem took shape in my backyard, straining to see meteors against a bright moon and city lights. Everything fell into place as I contemplated relationships in terms of astronomy." He lives in Wisconsin.

**Steve Eng** (1979), in addition to being a poet is also a critic and scholar of fantasy poetry. His collection *Yellow Rider and Other Fantasy Poems* spans his career. He also writes biographies and about drama. He lives in Tennessee.

**Helen Ehrlich** (1984) explores pre- and post-human Earth in her two sonnets. Science often provides a poet with and Ehrlich makes excellent use of extrapolating anthropology into formal verse. She lives in Arizona.

**Suzette Haden Elgin** (1988) is the founder of the Science Fiction Poetry Association. Her fiction includes The Ozark Trilogy and The Native Tongue Trilogy. In addition she has written the non-fiction *Gentle Art of Verbal Self-Defense*. In addition to numerous other projects she runs The Ozark Center for Language Studies, which, in addition to providing information about linguistics, is dedicated to reducing violence in the U.S.A. She lives in Arkansas.

**John M. Ford** (1989) has won the World Fantasy Award twice, including for this Rhysling winning poem. In addition to his fiction he has designed games and won three Origins Awards given by the Game Designer's Guild..

**Robert Frazier** (1980, 1989, 1994) lives in Massachusetts. Among his many accomplishments in the field Frazier has edited the magazines *Star*Line* and *T.A.S.P.: The Anthology of Speculative Poetry*. He is the editor of an early and important anthology of speculative poetry *Burning With a Vision*. His poetry continually shows an intelligent and modern approach to poetry. He is also a critic and historian of the field.

**Terry A. Garey** (1997) lives in Minnesota where she cans tomatoes every year. She says of her poem: "I originally wrote the poem to please my friend Karen. Then Eleanor Arnason had heard about a SF cookbook. "Why don't you send that tomato poem?" she asked. I told her it wasn't SF. "Oh, put some UFOs or something in it," she replied. So I did, and it was a much better poem. It was the only poem in the anthology. Never underestimate a potential market and always listen to your friends." She is the editor of the anthology *Time Frames* and was the first poetry editor for *Tales of the Unanticipated*.

**Theodora Goss** (2004) resides in Massachusetts. She is currently working on her Ph.D. in English literature. She has taught courses on fantasy and is influenced by Eastern European fairy tales in her writing, which has appeared in numerous magazines and anthologies.

**John Grey** (1998) lives in Rhode Island. He says of his poem: "Perhaps its theme owes something about this peculiar tendency of mine as a kid to wonder about the home-life of the villains in all those b movies an t.v. shows I used to dote upon. What kind of families did they come from? What do their mothers think of their plot to blow up the planet?"

**Joe Haldeman** (1984, 1991, 2001) About "Saul's Death" he says: "I wrote almost nothing but poetry until I started writing fiction in the late 60's. When I started writing for a living, I made a conscious decision to stop writing poetry . . . Sometime around 1980 I began to regret the decision, and thought I would ease back into poetry by writing a long narrative poem . . . At first I'd intended to do it along the lines of "The Rime of the Ancient Mariner." But I . . . came across Ezra Pound's fierce "Sestina: Altaforte," and the next day I was off and running." Of "Eighteen Years Old . . . " he says it was "to answer an assignment in Ottone Riccio's workshop. 'A woman loses an earring. It rolls behind a couch and is forgotten.'" He has won both the Nebula and Hugo Award for his prose. He lives in Florida.

**Andrew Joron** (1978, 1980, 1986) lives in California. He was the editor of the influential poetry magazine *Velocities* and is a critic as well as a poet. He works as a freelance proofreader and library assistant. He is also is a translator of German poetry and philosophy.

**Ursula K. Le Guin** (1982) is one of the most respected writers in American literature. She has continued to write poetry (six volumes) along with adult fiction, children's books, essays and criticism. She has won five Nebula and Hugo Awards, the World Fantasy Award twice, National Book Award as well as numerous others awards. She has been a finalist for the American Book Award and the Pulitzer Prize. She is the daughter of anthropologist Alfred Kroeber and the writer Theodora Kroeber, author of *Ishi.* She lives in Oregon.

**Geoffrey A. Landis** (2000) was a member of the Rover team on the successful Mars Pathfinder mission, and was selected to be a member of the science team on the Mars 2003 Exploration Rovers Mission. He says of his poetry "I first took poetry seriously at Clarion, where Joe Haldeman gave us an assignment to write a science fiction poem. To my surprise, I rather liked the poem that resulted. Since then I have written poetry on and off." Of his poem he says: "I've been fascinated by the contradictions and potentials inherent in time travel . . . I got thinking what would happen if you could buy a time machine at K-Mart, and what sort of everyday, mundane stuff people might use it for. And, as it happened, Christmas was just over, so it went from there." He lives in Ohio.

**Alan P. Lightman** (1983) was educated at Princeton and the California Institute of Technology. He has taught at Harvard and has been involved with the PBS TV shows Sesame Street and Smithsonian World. His essays have appeared in Smithsonian, The New York Times and the Boston Globe. His novels include: Einstein's Dreams (which has been translated into thirty languages), The Diagnosis and Reunion. He lives in Massachussetts.

**David Lunde** (1992, 1995) lives in Oregon. He says of "Song of the Martian Cricket": "I was driving home when a particularly full moon rose over the hills, lighting up the vineyards interspersed with patches of woods. I was wishing my wife were there with me to enjoy it and missing her badly. Before my journey ended, I had managed to compose most of the poem, transposing my longings to a science-fictional setting." Of "Pilot, Pilot" he says "[it is] one of those infrequent and magical-seeming poems that came into one's head almost fully formed . . . the scene described in the poem came to me as a vivid mental image . . . about three in the morning—the same time my daughter was born!" He also notes that the poem is better understood in conjunction with other poems in the series.

**Rebecca Marjesdatter** (2000) lives in Minnesota. She says of her poem: "The title is entirely unrelated to Wicce, but the first verse is autobiographical. Around age 11-14, I read fantasy novels in that same modestly obsessive fashionLe Guin, Lewis, McKillip, Tolkien, De Lint, et. al.—always hoping something magical might someday happen. Fortunately, I learned to make my own magic, of various kinds, and with happier results than in the poem. So, it's about enchantment, creativity, immortality in art, and Poesque creepiness. Is it any wonder I'm proud?"

**Patrick McKinnon** (1990) is the co-founder and Director of Poetry Harbor, a thriving literary organization based in Duluth, MN, which produces poetry performances, published books, chapbooks, and the magazine, North Coast Review. Patrick's poetry has appeared in more than 600 publications worldwide. He has over 15 collections of published poetry and has given more than 100 performances of his work. He has twice been awarded a Minnesota State Arts Board Poetry Fellowship from the McKnight Foundation. He is also the Senior Editor for the literary magazine Poetry Motel.

**David Memmott** (1991) is the founder of Wordcraft Publishing. He says of his poem: " . . . [it] evolved from my desire to write a first-person poem in which the "I" was a character outside myself... for sometime a line in my journal—"They were already dead when I got there"—kept running through my mind [as] a good line in a poem about extinct species." Combine that with the irony of cryonics company logo using a Phoenix rising from the ashes and an article on the five great extinctions and you have "the kind of fusion that is possible in speculative poetry: a fusion of science, science fiction, poetic tradition, mythology, religion, politics, fantasy and history in such a way as to resonate into dimensions beyond anything we could have plotted-out . . . " He lives in Oregon.

**Susan Palwick** (1986) is an Assistant Professor of English at the University of Nevada, Reno, where she teaches writing and literature. Her first novel, Flying in Place, won the Crawford Award for Best First Fantasy Novel, presented annually by the International Association for the Fantastic in the Arts. She has also been nominated for The World Fantasy Award.

**Peter Payack** (1980) is a widely published poet and writer including multiple appearances in *The Paris Review*, *Rolling Stone*, *The Cornell Review* and *Asimov's Science Fiction.* Payack is the inventor of the world-renowned Stonehenge Watch™, an infinitesimal replica of the megaliths at Stonehenge inside of an old-fashioned pocket watch, which can be used as a shadow clock to tell time, mark the seasons and predict eclipses. He has published 6 books, the latest, *Blanket Knowledge* (Zoland Books). When not writing poetry or inventing new things, he can be observed coaching The Cambridge Rindge & Latin School wrestling team, teaching at Berklee College of Music and University of Massachusetts Lowell or running. He has run 24 marathons, including 13 Boston Marathons!

**Jonathan V. Post** (1987) is, in addition to being an author, an editor, scientist, and business executive with 20 years in the space program. He teaches at Woodbury University in Burbank, CA. He has almost 900 publications, presentations, and broadcasts, some with Sir Arthur C. Clarke, Dr. Isaac Asimov, Ray Bradbury, and Nobel Laureate (physics) Richard Feynman. His website, magicdragon.com includes an outline of SF poetry history. He lives in California.

**Dan Raphael** (1995) says of his poem "I was surprised when this poem won the award, as I don't label my work. On the other hand, science and speculation are important to my work, part of the vision that language brings out in my writing. The Tao of Physics was a very influential book for me, in that it confirmed a lot of thoughts I was already having about the relationship of science and mysticism." He also notes his poetry his meant to be read aloud and is key to his work. Born in Pittsburgh and schooled at Cornell and Bowling Green State, he now lives in Oregon. His most recent books are *When a Flying City Falls* (nine muses books) and *Showing Light a Good Time* (Jazz Police.)

**John Calvin Rezmerski** (1987) resides in Minnesota where he teaches at Gustavus Adolphus College. With fellow Rhysling winners Terry Garey, Rebecca Marjesdatter and Laurel Winter, he is a member of Lady Poetesses From Hell, who perform poetry readings around the Midwest.

**Charles Saplak** (2003) He says of the collaborative poem done with Mike Allen: " . . . [it] was cooked up over some mediocre bookstore cappuccinos. Eventually we had a poem which dealt with an immortal dragon, waiting for a succession of slayers, doomed to remember each 'lifetime.' At first, that's all it was, but sometimes an idea won't let go. We were compelled to go back . . . to flesh out the history of said dragon. So the process actually went backwards in time so to speak, a kind of psychic archaeology." He lives in Virginia.

**Lawrence Schimel** (2002) is the author and editor of over forty-five titles. His work has been translated into over fifteen languages and included in over one hundred anthologies. He is a member of the National Book Critics Circle and the Academy of American Poets. He lives in Madrid and New York.

**Lucius Shepard** (1988) published his first book in 1967, a volume of poetry. In addition to traveling the world and working in many types of jobs, he has won numerous awards for his prose including the Locus Award and World Fantasy Award. He lives in Washington State.

**Margaret B. Simon** (1996) is currently, for the second time, the editor of *Star*Line*, the journal of the Science Fiction Poetry Association. She has been actively involved in promoting poetry being an important reason for the Horror Writers of America awarding a Stoker for best poetry collection. She says of her poem: "I recall the joy I had reading W. Gregory Stewart's 'the button and what you know' . . . [and] I decided I would write a long poem myself, which I'd never tried before. I didn't know how it would end, but it unfolded as if it were already *there* as I wrote. I have written no long poems since and don't know that I ever shall." In 2001, Marge Simon married Bruce Boston. She has retired from teaching and devotes her time to writing and illustration.

**W. Gregory Stewart** (1987, 1992, 1994, 1997) was born in Toronto, but grew up in Florida and Arizona. He is involved as a poetry judge and volunteers time at an experimental elementary school helping with children's poetry workshops. In addition to the Rhysling he has won a Fluvanna Award for light verse. He believes that if one picture is worth a thousand words, then it is the goal of poetry to even up the odds. He lives in California.

**Sonya Taaffe** (2003) has an addiction to mythology and folklore. Her first pieces were published in 2001; since then, her short fiction and poetry have appeared in numerous magazines. She says of her work: "Liminal spaces fascinate me. So do the figures who inhabit these regions in-between, who transgress and transform and encompass contradictions; or simply, like good speculative work, demonstrate that the world is a much more possible place than you think. This, Matlacihuatl—*Mujer enredadora,* Entangling Woman—does very well. I encountered her in the spring of my third year at college, while rehearsing for a recital and reading Lewis Hyde's *Trickster Makes This World;* three sentences would not get out of my head, and a few days later she was in this poem. Thanks to Luis Yglesias, Peter Gould, and Alison

McGurrin. They know why." She is currently pursuing a Ph.D. in Classical Studies at Yale University.

**Jeff VanderMeer** (1994) says his poem: " . . . had two sources of inspiration—first the songs of Freedy Johnson and second, a short story of mine also called 'Flight . . . ' I was stuck on the short story, which is told from the point of view of the guard in the poem, so I decided to write from the perspective of the prisoner, and out came the poem. Because the poem made me understand the very simplified and ironic world of the prisoner, I was then able to complete the short story. I do not write poetry very much, but when I do, it is to catch an instant of transformation, that critical moment in which something of great beauty and yet great pain is happening or is about to happen." He lives in Florida.

**William John Watkins** (2002) is a founding faculty member of Brookdale Community College. He has published over 400 poems and has won The Hellas Award. He has also placed in the top ten of the *Asimov's* Annual Reader's Poll fifteen times and is a Nebula Award finalist. He lives in New Jersey, where he races motorcycles with his son.

**Laurel Winter** (1998, 1999) lives in Minnesota. Her poems won back-to-back Rhyslings and Asimov's Reader's Polls. She says of her poems: "'why goldfish . . . ' came out of the ether. I really have no clue, except that I am exceedingly odd. 'egg horror poem' originated while my kids and I were decorating Easter eggs with colored pencils instead of dye. I grabbed a regular graphite pencil and started writing a little story on an egg—had to write "continued on next egg," as it was too long. I liked it, so I typed it up and put in line breaks. It has been pointed out to me at cons that I wrote a poem from the POV of eggs on the corpse of an egg, which is rather creepy . . . ."

**Gene Wolfe** (1978) is the first winner of a Rhysling for Long Poem. He was also an early supporter of the SFPA. Wolfe graduated with a degree in engineering from the University of Houston. His prose has won him two Nebula Awards, two World Fantasy Awards and many other awards, including World Fantasy Award for Lifetime Achievement. Born in New York, he now lives in Illinois.

**Jane Yolen** (1993) is a well-known poet, children's book author, editor, and novelist. She is a professional storyteller and has been called "America's Han Christian Andersen." Her books have won, among others, the World Fantasy Award, the Society of Children's Book Writers Award and the Daedalus Award. She lives in Massachusetts.